MY WAR WITH BASEBALL

ILLUSTRATED BY BILL BALLANTINE

MY WAR WITH BASEBALL

Rogers Hornsby and Bill Surface

FOREWORD BY CASEY STENNGEL

Originally published in 1962

All rights reserved. This book, or parts thereof, must not be reproduced in any form without permission.

ACKNOWLEDGMENTS

The efforts of many went into the publication of this book. Thanks go to Jack Geoghegan, Charles Dwoskin, H. W. Kellick, Dick Denny, Betsy Cullen, Mrs. Rogers Hornsby, Ellis Amburn, and to True magazine for permission to reprint material contained in an article we did for them.

Contents

Foreword by CASEY STENGEL 9
1. Why I'm Ol' Hard-Boiled Hornsby 13
2. My Forty-Eight Years in Baseball 35
3. The Game's Not the Same 57
4. There Won't Be Any More .400 Hitters 79
5. The General Problem—General Managers 95
6. Don't Kill the Umpire 111
7. Salaries and Bonuses 139
8. We Sold You 161
9. You've Got to "Cheat" to Win 173
10. Bean Balls and Spitters 193
11. Nobody Wins the World Series 207
12. How to Get in the Doghouse 223
13. My All-Time Team 239
14. Cleaning the Bases 265

Foreword
by CASEY STENGEL

ROGERS HORNSBY was the greatest right-handed hitter who ever played second base in anybody's league. No doubt about it. How am I so sure? Well, during the years Mr. Hornsby was burning up the National League with his bat, I played outfield for the Dodgers, Pirates, Phillies, Giants and Braves. And I had to chase an awful lot of those balls Mr. Hornsby hit out there. Helped keep me in shape.

Later on, when I managed the Braves from 1938-43, I heard one of my players complain that the ball park where we played was impossible to hit in. "Could be," I told him, "but this is the place where Mr. Hornsby played ball in 1928 for the Braves and he happened to hit .387—he was managing the team most part of the season, too—and that won him the National League batting championship."

Rogers, though, didn't go for any clown stuff. He'd just sit by himself in the dugout, and when he went to the plate he must have thought that this was war and his bat was his rifle or something. If it had of been war, I'm sure Rogers would have won all kinds of medals. He won all kinds of things as a hitter, including six batting championships in a row.

Now most people, when they talk about Hornsby, just talk about his hitting. Especially those three years he hit over .400. Well, in my opinion, he was just amazing on the double play, was just terrific as a runner, and his judgment on the playing field was just keen.

He isn't a fellow who goes around shaking hands and saying nice things about people unless he means it. He said what he thought. He lost a lot of managing jobs. He had a number of arguments—public and private. But he never backed up from anybody on the baseball field or in the front office.

MY WAR WITH BASEBALL

1. Why I'm Ol' Hard-Boiled Hornsby

WHEN you hit sixty-five—retirement age—you start thinking about all the things you've done. You're ashamed of some things—everybody is—but you're awful proud of most of your life. My life has been professional baseball since 1914 and I don't have to be ashamed of my record. I had a lifetime batting average of .358 in the major leagues, won the National League batting championship 7 times and batted over .400 in three seasons. By the time I was thirty years old, I had managed a team to the World Series championship—the 1926 St. Louis Cardinals. I also managed the St. Louis Browns, Chicago Cubs, Boston Braves, Cincinnati Reds, and was acting manager of the New York Giants. I've been a coach, too. And now I'm a batting coach.

More than all my honors in 48 years of baseball I'm proudest of the fact that I am not a baseball hypocrite. I've never had to worry about anybody telling anybody else what I said behind their back. I've never taken back anything I ever said and I've never failed to say exactly—

Baseball is a good show itself. You don't need clowns, midgets acrobats, and monkeys.

and I mean exactly—what I was thinking. To everybody—from the owner to the bat boy.

When I was a little boy in north Fort Worth, Texas, my mother started me in baseball by sewing me a uniform. Then she taught me not to drink or smoke, and above everything to always tell the truth. Unfortunately not everybody likes to hear the truth. I called a spade a spade, and sometimes I think this got me in more trouble than I would have gotten in if I had been a drinker. That's why I haven't got a high-paying major-league baseball job now. I didn't "yes" anybody. Truth hurts most people. It shortened my managing career in the major leagues. I'd rather have a modest job—or no job—and be truthful and satisfied, than be a frustrated, scared liar with a good managing job.

I'm not known anywhere as "beloved," or "the grand old man of baseball." My wife has a barrel in storage filled with some of my clippings. There are articles like "Hard-Boiled Hornsby Starts in on Another Team," and "The Bluntest, Toughest, Stubbornest Manager of All Time." There are stories on guys who claimed playing under me was like being in reform school. There are articles accusing me of such crimes as betting on horse races and talking back to important baseball people. Why couldn't I talk back to important baseball people? I had batting averages of .424 and .403 in successive seasons and was the batting champion for 6 straight years.

I never deliberately tried to get anybody mad at me as a player or manager. It's lots easier to get people mad at managers. I was paid as a manager to make decisions to win ball games. I had the guts to believe my decisions were right, and I stood up for them. I never second-guessed umpires, my coaches, my players or the owners.

My War with Baseball

At the same time, however, I wasn't a diplomat. I was either on one fence or the other. I didn't want anybody coming up, throwing their arms around me and kissing me because we won. Or maybe because I agreed with them. I didn't stand for any griping, crying, whining, alibiing or phony stuff from my players.

They claim I was stuck up as a player. Like hell I was. I wanted to be a success at playing ball. I didn't want to tell funny stories or brag back and forth. I wanted to concentrate on the game. If anybody wanted to talk about the pitcher we were facing, or offer some suggestions, I was tickled to death to talk. But no bull.

I've been called a sour old man as a manager because I didn't jump up and down and slap backs after somebody hit a home run or we won a game. Hell, that's what we were getting paid to do. I know most of the players I managed didn't have the ability I had. All I ever demanded as a manager was the same thing I always gave—an honest, aggressive effort.

No player owed me anything as a manager. He owed it first to the fans and second to himself to give a 100 percent effort. The players all received damn good salaries for playing baseball—not spending the summer running a bowling alley or telling jokes when they should be concentrating on the game; not slipping under the runway of the dugout where half the kids in the stands can see their idols sneaking around like spies and smoking. Guys weren't supposed to sit around talking about picking up women after the game.

What's more I didn't want any beer drinking or big card games for money in my clubhouse before a game. They didn't build clubhouses for beer parties and card

Why I'm Ol' Hard-Boiled Hornsby

games. If they did they would have put in fancy gambling tables and a bar—and hired a union bartender. Clubhouses are supposed to be used to talk in about how to beat somebody in baseball. The way I looked at it pro baseball isn't a recreation like fishing or sun-bathing. Players get paid to win, and it was my job as manager to see that they tried to.

If players thought I was mean they should have spent a little time under John McGraw when he was managing the New York Giants. He was ten times tougher than me. He'd fine players for speaking to somebody on the other team. Or being caught with a cigarette. He'd walk up and down the dugout and yell "Wipe those damn smiles off your face."

He'd warn players against becoming buddy-buddy with sports writers. One rookie was really scared. When a writer asked "Are you married?" the rookie answered, "You'd better ask Mr. McGraw."

Hell, McGraw even accused me of deliberately missing a ground ball. That got me so hot I started hollering right back in his face. He liked that kind of stuff. He just didn't make curfew rules and put the players on their honor to obey them like I did. Every night at exactly 11:30 you could hear a knock on your door. It was the Giants' trainer and he was following McGraw's orders to personally see that everybody was in bed. When McGraw said everybody was to eat breakfast at 9 o'clock that meant you had better have your order in to the waitress *by* 9 A.M.

But anyway, I'm not trying to glorify myself. I wasn't trying to lead all my players to a revival after the game. Their personal lives were their own after the game—the same as I wanted for myself—but I was going to make damn sure there wouldn't be anything else on their minds during the game. Not a thing but baseball. I managed like I played—until I got fired for saying no when I meant no. Anybody who hired me as a manager knew he wasn't getting a yes man. He should have—I had enough big public arguments about it.

I never deliberately tried to embarrass a player in front of the whole team for making a human error. I made errors, too. But if there were instances where I knew a player needed to be bawled out for doing something he shouldn't, I didn't think it was necessary to call him into the restroom and whisper to him.

One day in 1935 when I was manager of the St. Louis Browns our train was just pulling out of St. Louis and headed for Cleveland when I noticed that Dick Kauffman, one of my leading pitchers, had obviously spent too much time in a saloon.

So I called him into the drawing room and said, "Dick, you're not in any condition to go on this trip. You'd better get off at the next stop which is Belleville, Illinois, then go back to the hotel and tell Mr. McAvoy [the general manager] that I sent you home."

"Well," Dick said, the way most people talk when they aren't feeling any pain, "I'm not getting off."

He argued a helluva lot more. Then I said, "This train is going to stop at Belleville and somebody is going to get off."

He got wise and made a lot of noise. We started out in a wrestling match and had a big fight. He got off at

Why I'm Ol' Hard-Boiled Hornsby

Belleville. A manager has to have discipline and respect or he doesn't have a team.

They say I was "too different" as a manager. I wasn't trying to be different. I wanted to be right. I wasn't managing scared. Take today's managers, for instance. You'll see some of them spending as much time on the pitcher's mound as the relief pitcher. They're just out there to show the fans who the manager is—or to get on nationwide TV. Or to impress the club owners. I always discussed how to pitch to the hitters before a game. After a guy knocks one out of the park it sure as hell doesn't do any good to hold a big fancy conference on the mound to talk about "how we should have pitched to him."

Most times a manager is just inviting trouble by going to the mound if he definitely has made up his mind about changing pitchers. There isn't a pitcher alive who ever wanted to be taken out. Some pitchers can be so tired they're practically rolling the ball in and then when the manager asks how they feel, they'll sound like a politician a week before election day. Pitchers always claim they're as fresh as the minute they started.

Look what happened in the fourth game of the 1957 World Series between the Milwaukee Braves and the New York Yankees. Warren Spahn, the greatest pitcher in the game today, had the Yankees beat 4-1, but was tired in the ninth inning. Two Yankees got on base. Fred Haney, the Braves manager, went out to the mound, and a lot of people say he had his mind made up about taking out Spahn. But Spahn stayed in and the next batter, Elston Howard, hit a home run that tied up the game.

I got burned the same way early in my managing career and it sure as hell taught me a lesson. When I was

My War with Baseball

playing manager of the 1925 St. Louis Cardinals I'd just trot in from second base to talk to a pitcher. Arthur Reinhart was my pitcher, and I had definitely decided he was losing his stuff and finished for the day. As soon as I got to the mound I heard him begging, "Let me just pitch to this one hitter. I can get him out."

Well, I always liked to be fair and didn't like to take players out of a game unless absolutely necessary. "All right, Art," I said, "pitch to this batter."

The batter knocked the very first pitch over on Grand Avenue for a home run with the bases loaded. I made up my mind then and there that if I continued to manage anywhere I wouldn't go out to the mound to take out a pitcher. If I ever went out it was only to quiet him down or to change strategy. I just waved to the bullpen for a new pitcher. I know that didn't look very polite, but I didn't think it was necessary to go out and hand the guy the ball and carry the other guy off on my shoulders. In my opinion he ought to have a damn good lecture—or even a kick in the rear end—for getting the bases full or getting into the position of having to be taken out.

So I consider many of today's big strategy meetings as phony. And I never went for anything phony. That goes for all that silly side-show stuff.

Baseball is our national pastime and always has been. It's a good show itself. People used to fight their way into a ball park to see a good game—18 men fighting the hell out of each other to win. You don't need midgets, side shows or exploding scoreboards to draw people. If the fans wanted to see this kind of stuff they wouldn't come to a baseball game and hope to see a couple of monkeys chasing a jeep between innings. They'd go to Ringling

Why I'm Ol' Hard-Boiled Hornsby

Brothers' Circus. Or some tent carnival where you can see hoochy-coochy dancers on the side.

Guys like Bill Veeck call this color. Color, hell. What's more colorful than the home team hitting a home run or beating somebody? What's more colorful than a winning team? The World Series isn't hurting for color, is it?

Baseball fans don't drive hundreds of miles to see a bunch of clowns. Ballplayers don't make good clowns. Joe Garagiola, an ex-ballplayer, made some money by writing a book called *Baseball Is a Funny Game*. I congratulate Joe on the success of his book, but baseball is not, in my opinion, a funny game.

When Veeck hired me to manage the St. Louis Browns in 1952, I laid the cards on the table. I told him I wouldn't permit any circus acrobats coaching at first or third base; no midgets batting, like he had had the year before. No side shows in the middle of the diamond. I also told him he wasn't going to tell me how to run my personal life. I told him he wasn't going to tell me how to manage the team. I told him I was shooting for the first division. We agreed on everything and signed a three-year contract at $36,000 a year.

We opened spring training in El Centro, California, and about the first thing I saw was two carloads of those little old midgets driving up and running out on the field where we were trying to get in shape to play major league baseball. Those midgets would really help us beat the Yankees, wouldn't they? My message was simple and loud: "Get the hell out of here and don't come back. We don't want that kind of stuff around here."

One of those little old midgets just stared at me. So I picked him up by the seat of the pants and collar and threw him over the railing. I wasn't going to put up with that nonsense. We didn't have any more midgets around after that. But of course I didn't stay for all three years.

We were playing the Yankees in the first game of a double-header in Yankee Stadium in 1952 when Tommy Byrne of the Browns hit a high foul ball and third baseman Gil McDougald leaned against the stands and almost caught it. Then umpire Art Paparella ruled interference on the play and called Byrne out. I was standing right there, coaching at third base, and it was a call that probably could have been described as a little questionable. But it was strictly an umpire's judgment play and you can't protest that. It says so right in the book.

But Veeck was listening to the game on the radio a thousand miles away in St. Louis and thought he saw the play better than the umpire and everybody else. He telephoned Bill Durney, our traveling secretary, and ordered him to tell me to protest the game.

"Look," I told Durney down in the dugout, "you just telephone Mr. Veeck right back collect and tell Mr. Veeck that I'll tell the umpire that Mr. Veeck is protesting, not me. I'm not going to make an ass out of myself like that. This is two hours later and we're protesting."

Then I went to the plate umpire and told him that Veeck was protesting, not me. Some managers, I guess, would have accepted those terms and gone right on drawing their salary for being an errand boy. But when I got back to the Hotel Commodore I telephoned Bill and said, "Mr. Veeck, you'd better make up your mind whether you want to manage the club or want me to manage. There isn't going to be any half and half. I want to get this straightened out once and for all. If you're a better manager in Yankee Stadium from St. Louis than I am in Yankee Stadium, then you take the job." When we got to Boston the next day Veeck was waiting for me in the Kenmore Hotel. We got it straightened out. We parted company.

I was in the first year of a written contract for three years at $36,000 a year. Legally I was entitled to my salary in full for the rest of the season and the complete 1953-54 seasons. Like managers get when they're fired. But I had voluntarily told Veeck that if we didn't get along I would give him back half of the money. It was only a verbal agreement and I had a legal, written agreement for my salary.

I said, "My word is my bond, Bill. Even though we're breaking up, you don't have to pay me in full for the third year."

I could have been $18,000 richer today if I had taken the money. Veeck really must have appreciated it. The newspapers only announced that he paid me off in full, and Veeck even claimed the players were so relieved and grateful to him for firing me that they all chipped in, went downtown and bought an "Emancipation Trophy," had it engraved and presented it to him from the bottom of their hearts. Veeck said it was for being the greatest liberator since Lincoln freed the slaves. It was one of the biggest bush-league stunts I ever saw. Some of the players told me later that they were embarrassed because they knew nothing about it until the secretary brought the trophy in to Veeck—on his own orders—and handed it to one of the players to present to Veeck. So you can see that anybody who loves and respects baseball like I do isn't going to stand for this silly stuff.

My War with Baseball

One of the reasons given for the St. Louis Browns' miserable showing was my clubhouse rules. I didn't allow beer and I supposedly had the players so nervous they couldn't play ball. 'Course, most of them couldn't play anyway. They were the real clowns. I never once interfered with their private lives because I respect those as much as anyone. I never told anyone what to do after a game, except observe the training curfew. I always maintained there was enough time after the game for recreation. Some guys got their recreation by drinking, chasing women, or ruining their eyes watching movies. I thought all of these things were of no help to me. I picked horse racing—something that millions of people enjoy every year—as my recreation. Sometimes I think I would have satisfied more people and things would have gone smoother if I had been a Peeping Tom or a pool shark.

Some baseball hypocrites regard horse racing as something shady, but I saw President Eisenhower and his wife at Belmont Park and they didn't look ashamed of themselves. They waved to half the country on TV. Presented a trophy, too. Anyway, 75 percent of the big-league players today kill time at race tracks. I didn't have all my run-ins for going to races. Trouble was, I didn't deny it or sneak around after dark.

One day when I was playing for the Cards, Judge Kenesaw Mountain Landis, the commissioner of baseball, told me to come to his office in Chicago. His office looked like a federal court. Some guy was taking a transcript. Then the Judge started. "Mr. Hornsby," he said, "I've received varied reports and strong rumors that you bet on race horses."

"Well, Judge Landis," I answered, "they aren't just rumors. I bet on horses. That's my only recreation."

Why I'm Ol' Hard-Boiled Hornsby

"Then I'm ordering you to stop," he snapped back. "It's gambling."

"I know it's gambling," I said, "and baseball and gambling don't mix. That's why I never play cards in the clubhouse with the other players. They're playing for money. I wait till later and maybe pick out a horse."

"That's some excuse," the Judge said. "And you're going to stop."

"Look at it this way," I said. "I don't drink, smoke or go to the movies. Don't even read anything but the baseball boxscores. Don't even go to the races over once or twice a year. I can relax by betting a horse now and then."

"It's gambling," the Judge said, shaking his finger. "It's gambling."

"Well, I know it's gambling," I said just as strongly. "But so is the stock market. You can't tell me it's worse to gamble with my own money than it is to gamble on the stock market. Like you putting money that belongs to baseball in the stock market and losing."

That ended the conversation real quick. The Judge felt it was all right to criticize me for gambling, but he didn't like to be reminded that he had gambled with other people's money and lost everything in the 1929 stock market crash. Needless to say, people didn't see any pictures in the paper of the Judge and me hugging each other at the ball park.

I always felt like Bill Klem, the great umpire, did about horse racing. "I've seen baseball drive people to drinking," Bill has said, "and I've seen it drive some people nuts. I can bring in guys for proof. But I can umpire a half dozen of the toughest and tightest games in the world—go out to the races—and not even remember there was a ball game. I was a better umpire that way."

I realized then and now, of course, that I could have had lots more friends and better jobs by denying I ever looked at a horse. But I live with myself. I hate phonies. I never denied it the next time I was called on the carpet about it either. That was in August of 1937, when I was managing the St. Louis Browns. Donald Barnes had just bought controlling interest in the Browns. He had made his money in the small-loan business and was trying to expand. Even sold me some stock on time. I still owed him about $6,000.

And I won about $6,000 too, real quick on the horses. We were playing the Red Sox in St. Louis when I got over a good three-horse parlay. The horses were all given to me by a handicapper, who sent me a telegram. After I got the wire I went to a phone booth across the street from the ball park—now this was a long time before the game—and made a big parlay in St. Louis. Then I called a bookmaker in Chicago and made another parlay on the same three horses.

I must have had a grin on my face or something. Then I ran into Bobo Newsome of the Red Sox after leaving the phone booth. And since Bobo knew we both bet the horses, he grabbed the telegram out of my hand and found out what horses I bet and went into another restaurant where you could place a horse bet as easily as you could get a cheeseburger. I had got Bobo into the big leagues by drafting him out of the Pacific Coast League and even though he had been sold we knew each other's habits pretty well.

Why I'm Ol' Hard-Boiled Hornsby

Newsome didn't bet as much as I did, but I understand he did sort of "clean up"—for Bobo that is. Naturally he was a little excited and bought a few drinks after the game. No doubt he talked about getting over the parlay. Probably told the guys where he got the horses, because he liked to joke and cut up. One of the people who happened to be in the place was Bill DeWitt, who was the general manager for Barnes. Word quickly got back to Barnes that I had hit a pretty good horse.

I did, as a matter of fact, hit the books pretty hard that day and they paid off with a check. I told them to give me a cashier's check for $6,000 even, so I could just endorse it and pay off Barnes for the stock I bought.

Barnes had heard about my winning horses and was sitting all propped up when I handed him the check. He asked me where-in-the-hell did I get the check and I told him "Where-in-the-hell do you think I got it? I don't remember you making this an extra payday."

He just threw up his hands, which meant, as far as I was concerned, that everything was settled. But it wasn't. The next day I was called into Barnes' office. DeWitt was sitting alongside him. Barnes tried to look a little tough or bossy, then said, "This check has been traced to a bookie. We don't take that kind of money around here."

"Don't take that kind of money?" I hollered. "Whatta you mean anyway? I won it fair and square."

"Fair and square from a bookie?" he said.

"Hell, I never promised anybody I wouldn't play horses. You know that. So I hit one. That money is as good as the money you take from people in the loan-shark business. It's better than taking interest from widows and orphans."

I got fired. But I never knew a manager who didn't get fired at one time or another. And if anybody were to ask me today, I'd tell them the same thing. I still occasionally bet horses. Next to baseball it's the best sport going. Sport of kings.

Hell, I even got fired for *winning the pennant and World Series.* I wouldn't have gotten fired if I had let an owner run over me, but a man has to keep his pride and respect as a manager or he's finished. I was the playing manager of the 1926 St. Louis Cardinals, and the Cardinals won their first pennant and World Series in history by beating the New York Yankees in the series.

We were on our special train coming back to St. Louis after the series when Sam Breadon, the owner, called Bill Killefer, one of my coaches, into his drawing room and offered him my managing job for 1927. Bill turned down the job, and in being loyal like coaches should be came and told me what Breadon said.

I had been playing under the same salary for three years and didn't get a dime increase for managing the team. I didn't even get a pat on the back or new contract for taking over a team that was in the cellar and bringing them in fourth. And you'd think that after a player-manager wins the first pennant and world championship in the team's history the owner would have offered him more than a one-year contract. Later on Breadon only offered me a one-year contract. I refused to take it and asked for a three-year contract.

A year before, Breadon had turned down offers of around a quarter of a million dollars for me. But he was mad because I didn't like exhibition games when we were near a pennant, and of course wouldn't take a one-year contract. So he traded me to the New York Giants for Frankie Frisch, Pitcher Jimmy Ring and some money. That was the biggest disappointment I had in my life.

I owned 1,167 shares of Cardinal stock, which made me the second largest stockholder. Of course, John Heydler, the National League president, ruled that I couldn't play for the Giants and own stock in the Cardinals. It was the right decision, too.

I knew what my stock was worth and wasn't about to give it away. Mark Steinberg, a stockbroker friend of mine in St. Louis, appraised the stock and established a price of $120 a share. He even offered to pay Breadon $120 a share for any stock Breadon wanted to sell, so you can see that was a fair price.

The price was higher than it had been a year earlier, but Breadon didn't take into consideration the fact that the Cardinals had won the World Series and were a team that looked like they would be great for years. He only wanted to pay me $80,000 for all my stock. I thought the offer was ridiculous, and told him so, too. The deal dragged on during the spring. While I was in spring training with the Giants, Judge Landis telephoned me in Washington and told me to meet him in Pittsburgh and straighten out the deal. I had my lawyer there and didn't lower my price a nickel. Breadon didn't raise his offer a nickel either, and this went on until a couple of days before the 1927 season opened. Then John McGraw, the Giants' manager, told me to go to the Giants' office and sign some papers so I could play for them. The other 7 clubs all chipped in about $5,000 apiece to put with

My War with Baseball

Breadon's offer of $80,000 so that I could get my fair price. Despite having the biggest year in Cardinal history, Breadon didn't declare a dividend. But when he got all my stock he declared a dividend for himself.

I was happy at the chance of playing for McGraw. He must have liked me, too. When he was sick or had to be away, he made me playing manager. He told me to run the team like he would and that's exactly what I tried to do. One time when McGraw was sick and I was in charge of the Giants we lost a game to the Cubs in the ninth on an error by Travis Jackson, whom I consider a great competitor.

I don't like to lose any more than anybody else; neither did Jackson. I knew he felt bad about it, and it wasn't going to do any good to raise hell and beat my gums.

But a little guy named Jim Tierney cornered me and started chewing out Jackson in front of all the players. Tierney was the traveling secretary and a real close buddy of Charles Stoneham, owner of the Giants. So I started raising some hell myself—to Tierney. Like I should as manager of the team. "Dammit," I told Tierney, "you take care of the cabs and the hotel rooms and the tickets and we'll take care of playing ball."

Hell, he didn't have any business butting in like that. To make it even worse he didn't know much about baseball, either. I knew Tierney and Stoneham were close. I knew it before I yelled back, and I realized it even more afterward. I was traded at the end of the season, and if I had to face the same situation over again I'd say exactly the same thing. I contend a manager has to have the guts to take up for his players and to accept failures. I'd have

Why I'm Ol' Hard-Boiled Hornsby

been a damn poor manager if I had allowed people to bawl out my players in public.

Sportswriters claim I popped off too much. I didn't do any more talking than dozens of other guys. In fact, I didn't say anything until somebody asked me. Trouble was, I didn't go behind a tree and do any talking. Like "Don't say I said so, but this so-and-so fellow isn't any good." I talked out in the open.

The sportswriters, though, used all kinds of fancy words to describe my run-ins. If the stories were intended to upset me they certainly were wasted. I never read most of the stuff. I didn't care anything about publicity then. I don't now either.

Don't get the impression I'm knocking sports writers. I like many of them and always tried to be honest and aboveboard with them. The one thing that always peeved me, though, was reporters saying, "Now off the record, what do you think?"

I remember one night in 1927 when I was training with the Giants in Sarasota and centerfielder Edd Roush was holding out. McGraw had been quoted in the papers as saying Roush could hold out all year for all he cared. Many of the Giants' players didn't feel that way. I was one of them. Then a writer stopped me in the hotel lobby and said, "Now this isn't for publication, but what's the inside story on the Roush situation? What do you think about it? I won't tell McGraw what you say."

That burned me up. "Let's get this straight," I told him. "I don't talk 'not for publication.' You can put anything I say, any time you want, in the paper. What do I think of the outfield? It stinks, that's what. With Roush out of centerfield, all those clowns are running into each

My War with Baseball

other. McGraw hasn't asked me my opinion, but if he does I'll tell him exactly the same thing I told you."

Well, a few days later McGraw went to New York to talk to Stoneham about the Roush case and left me in charge of the team. Some writers were griping and ranting about McGraw being gone. One of them came up to me complaining. I simply said, "What difference does it make?"

"It makes a helluva lot of difference," the writer said. "Besides, ol' boy, you'd better quit popping off like that. Somebody might tell him what you said."

"Ol' buddy," I told him, "that's one darn thing I'll never have to worry about. I never say anything behind McGraw's back I wouldn't say to his face. You can even go tell him if you want to." I felt that was the only way to operate—not whispering behind people's backs. It's no fun to deny things.

And I was never nice to people when I didn't think I should be. Take the incident when I was managing the Cincinnati Reds in 1952. We were leading the Brooklyn Dodgers by 2 runs going into the last of the ninth inning. And for all practical purposes it looked like we had the game sewed up. Bud Podbielan, my best pitcher, was on the mound and was going real good. He walked a man on a questionable call, which happens to pitchers every day; then another Dodger got on base on an error, which certainly isn't any sign the pitcher is tiring. Then Junior Gilliam hit the very first pitch over the right-field fence for a home run to win the game 6-5. That was the only indication that Podbielan was weakening, and of course it was too late.

Why I'm Ol' Hard-Boiled Hornsby

We went into the dressing room feeling low. No doubt Bud felt the lowest. About that time Earl Lawson, a sportswriter for the Cincinnati *Times-Star*, ran into the club-house and over to me, practically waving his arms. "I thought you should have taken the pitcher out," he yelled at me loud enough for all the players to hear him.

So I used all the cuss words I ever knew and told Mr. Lawson to get the hell out of the clubhouse and never come back. What was I supposed to do? Let him humiliate my players, then give him a big cigar so he would write nice things about me? He could call me John Dillinger for all I cared. I wasn't running for public office.

Truthfully, I feel sports writers, or anybody else, don't have any business running into dressing rooms right after a team gets beat. You've been under a terrific strain and don't accept people as nicely as you normally do. It's no different than stepping on people's bare toes and asking them how they feel.

That's still the way I feel a clubhouse should be run. It's an old-fashioned way of thinking, I know, because they allow guys to barge in. It's a wonder that a manager doesn't pick up a bat and clobber a sportswriter or announcer someday. I wouldn't blame him.

So if that's being rough, tough, blunt, belligerent, hard boiled, outspoken, stubborn, old-fashioned and too demanding, then I don't mind being called rough, tough, blunt, belligerent, hard boiled, outspoken, stubborn, old-fashioned and too demanding. I don't feel anybody can ever honestly call me a loafer or two-faced.

2. My Forty-Eight Years in Baseball

I WAS born during the baseball season, April 27, 1896, on a small farm near a little West Texas town called Winters. My father, Edward Hornsby, was a farmer and cattle rancher. My mother was Mary Dallas Rogers Hornsby, and I was named "Rogers" after her. I was the youngest of five children—four boys and one girl—and we all loved to play baseball better than eat.

I didn't have much chance to play ball though, at first. My father died when I was two and we moved to Grandpa Rogers' farm about nine miles from Austin. Of course, you don't find enough kids around a farm to get up a full ball game. When I was five or six we moved into a house in north Fort Worth, so my older brothers could get jobs to support the family. I was around a lot of boys for the first time and I was able to get into some little kid games.

I got my first paying job when I was ten, working as a messenger boy for a packing house and being the bat boy for the baseball team. They didn't have players sticking to one position all the time, so by the time I was twelve I

was filling in on the team. Later on I got on an amateur team called the North Side Athletics.

My mind was made up now. I wanted to be a professional baseball player. Just like Ty Cobb, who was burning up the American League, or Honus Wagner, who was doing just as well in the National League.

I played ball every minute I could. My mother had never seen a professional game, but she understood how much I loved the sport and encouraged me by making my uniforms and some sliding pads out of quilt material.

When I was a freshman at North Side High School, Fort Worth, I played baseball and football. We had a pretty good football team—a boy named Bo McMillin was the fullback. I was the quarterback. But football was just something that kept me away from baseball. So I quit and played all the baseball I could.

My older brother, Everett, was a good spitball pitcher for Dallas in the Texas League, which then was a Class B league. Every time Everett's team came to Fort Worth he'd get me in the game free and I'd try to go down to the bench before the game to see him. When I was seventeen years old and weighed 135 and stood five foot eleven, Everett got me a tryout with Dallas. I was a shortstop. I never got into a game and was given my release after two weeks.

The only other chance I had was to play with a Dallas team was against the Boston Bloomer Girls. You were supposed to wear a wig and pretend you were a girl playing ball. It played in the Class D Texas-Oklahoma League. I didn't want any part of that. I caught a bus to Hugo, Oklahoma, got a tryout and made the team there. But the team didn't make it—financially, that is. Hugo folded six weeks after the season started. They sold my contract to Denison, which was in the same league, for $125. I didn't gain any weight and didn't set the world on fire. I batted only .232 in 113 games and made 45 errors. But I was playing professional baseball, and for me that's where life began.

1915—Denison played in the Western Association, which was Class D. I was the shortstop. The biggest excitement I had during spring training was playing against the St. Louis Cardinals' second team. We got beat, but that didn't matter so much. I got to see what I thought was a big-league team. It was my big break.

I weighed the same 135 pounds, but my batting average went up a little. I was hitting .277 when Roy Finley, who was the county attorney and president of the Denison team, called me aside in late August. Seems that Bob Connery, the scout who managed the Cardinals' second team in the game against us, liked the way I played and recommended me to the Cardinals. I heard the price for me was $500, but Connery later said it was $600.

They told me to meet the Cardinals in Cincinnati on September 1. I had never been North before, let alone a big city like Cincinnati. You didn't have a bunch of coaches helping the rookies. You had to scratch for everything you got; even the veterans on the teams were so jealous of their jobs that most of them wouldn't give you the time of day. In fact, I had to wait until all the regulars were finished before I got to take batting practice. Somedays I wouldn't have gotten any if Connery hadn't been around to pitch to me after the game.

I didn't get to play for a week after I joined the Cards, and it looked like I'd probably never get to play again.

My first game was in St. Louis against Cincinnati's Reds. I was, of course, scared to death at the plate. Fred Toney of the Reds struck me out the first two times I batted.

I played shortstop and even messed up my first fielding chance. Buck Herzog of the Reds broke for second base, trying to steal, and I covered second. Frank Snyder, our catcher, made a perfect throw to me, and we had Herzog out by 10 feet. Only I dropped the ball. Snyder really cussed me out in the dugout, too.

The first thing Miller Huggins, my manager, did afterward was suggest I change my batting stance. I was using the Fred Clarke model bat, named after the playing manager of the Pirates, and Huggins thought I was too light to swing from the end. "They throw a lot harder in the majors than Class D," he said, "and you don't have the strength to get the bat around. Here, try choking up on the bat."

It was a good suggestion. I got in 18 games and didn't make much of a reputation as a hitter. I batted .246 and apparently didn't impress Huggins with my hitting.

When the season ended (we finished sixth and the Phillies won the pennant) Huggins called me in his office and said, "I think I'm going to have to farm you out for next year."

I was just a country boy, with only three or four weeks in the big cities, so I took him at his word. I thought he meant a real farm and go to work. So I went down to my aunt and uncle's farm at Lockhart, Texas, and went to work. Also drank all the milk I could and tried to put on some weight.

1916—Went to San Antonio, Texas, where the Cardinals held spring training. They told me my salary would be $2,000 for the year if I made the club. But money wasn't important. It was obvious Huggins wasn't counting too heavily on me. He had one shortstop, Artie Butler, and had an option to buy Roy Corhan for $15,000 from the San Francisco Seals of the Pacific Coast League, which was 30 times as much as the Cards paid for me. I weighed 160 pounds now, and Huggins thought I had put on enough weight to swing natural again.

I was rooming with Corhan. He didn't hit very good, and I didn't do too bad since the extra weight helped me. Still I had a tough battle to become the shortstop. In the City Series with the St. Louis Browns a few days before the season opened, Corhan came up with a sore arm. And I got a chance to play shortstop in the City Series.

Every game gave me more confidence. And I had a funny experience here, too. We were playing against the Phillies and Grover Cleveland Alexander, who had won 30 games the year before and was to also win 30 this season. The Phils had a big enough lead so they didn't have to worry. Bill Killefer, who played with my brother in the Texas League, was catching.

"Say, kid," Killefer said to me when I came to bat, "here comes a good fast ball. Let's see what you can do with it."

I swung and hit it against the left-field fence for a double. I thought that if I can hit the great Alexander like this, then I should be able to hit anyone. I had loads of confidence after that.

I batted .313 in my first full big-league season. The Cardinals, who finished last, were weak everywhere and

I was used at every position except pitching and catching.

1917—Spent the winter working as a checker on the packing-house loading docks, where I started as a messenger boy, and counting the days until I would go to spring training with the Cardinals. Went to spring training in shape, and felt I had improved over the previous year. Batted .327, second highest in the National League, and led the League in triples with 17. My pay for the season was $3,000. The Cardinals finished third.

1918—Things were different this season. World War I had started. Jack Hendricks replaced Miller Huggins as manager. The Cardinals finished last. I was rejected by the Army because I was the sole support of my mother. Sprained my ankle and missed 35 games. Hit .281, which wasn't bad, but it was a bad year for me considering what I'd done the year before.

1919—Another new manager. Branch Rickey, a smart, polite man from the University of Michigan, who had managed the St. Louis Browns, replaced Hendricks. I had a lot more confidence and knew the good pitchers like Jim Vaughn of the Cubs and Alexander better. Hit 8 home runs and had a .318 batting average. Cardinals moved up a notch in the standings to seventh place.

1920—Got a pay raise—drawing $4,000 a year now. It was, of course, my biggest salary and it was my biggest year to date. I led the league in batting with a .370 average, in hits with 218, doubles with 44, and tied for the lead in runs batted in with 94. The Cardinals moved up another notch—now sixth.

1921—The Cardinals really moved up this year under Rickey, finishing third—7 games behind John McGraw

My War with Baseball

and his New York Giants. I got a big raise, about three times what I broke in with. It looked like I might hit .400 this season, but I missed it by two or three hits and had a .397 batting average, winning the National League championship for the second straight year. Statistics-wise, I led the league in runs (131), hits (235), doubles (44), runs batted in (126), and tied for the league lead in triples with 18. Had 21 home runs and didn't even win the home-run championship. Seems the ball was getting a little more lively, especially over in the American League where Ruth hit 59.

1922—The Cardinals finished in a tie with the Pirates for third place (the Giants won the pennant again) so even our last game of the season was important. We ended the season against the Cubs in Chicago's Wrigley Field. Jim Gould, a St. Louis sportswriter, called me aside and told me if I got 3 hits in the last game I could hit over .400. I was lucky enough to get them and won the batting championship—my third in a row—with a .401 average. I guess they must have used some of the new balls in the National League that year. I hit 42 home runs—more than doubled my best previous year—and wasn't trying to hit the long ball. I felt I was hitting the ball for base hits. Led the league in runs (141), hits (250), doubles (46), runs batted in (152), and even in fielding at second base with a .967 average.

1923—Since 1922 had been my best year and I had a higher batting average than anyone in modern Cardinal history, I got a good raise. Signed a three-year contract, covering '23, '24 and '25, for $18,000 a year.... The Cardinals finished down a little lower—fifth—and my batting average dropped a few points. It wasn't too bad—

.384—which won me the championship for the fourth year in a row. Only played in 107 games.

1924—Hustled on everything I hit. You make your breaks by hustling. I got some this way and probably other ways, too, because you have to be a little lucky to hit .414, which was my average for '24—the highest in modern history. Also led the league in doubles with 43 and hits (227). The Cardinals came in sixth; the Giants winning the pennant.

1925—During spring training in Stockton, California, I heard rumors that Sam Breadon, the Cardinal owner, wasn't pleased with Rickey's managing. Rickey said he'd heard the same thing. Then Rickey asked me to ask Breadon to give him another chance. I went to Breadon and said that Rickey was the smartest man in baseball. Breadon suggested I take the job as manager, but I wasn't interested. So he kept Rickey.

Things weren't going too well and a few weeks later Breadon called me to his hotel room in Stockton and offered me the job. I was only twenty-nine years old, had won 5 straight batting championships and still didn't want the job. I recommended that Breadon keep Rickey. I also told Breadon that if the Good Lord himself were to come down to California and manage this club, he couldn't do any better. It was a lousy team. On May 29 I was having breakfast by myself in the Hotel Schenley in Pittsburgh. Clarence Lloyd, the traveling secretary, told me that Breadon was in town and wanted to see me. When I passed by the table where Rickey and Coach Burt Shotton were sitting, Rickey stopped me.

"Breadon wants you to manage the team," Rickey said.

My War with Baseball

"I don't want to manage," I told him, "he knows that."

"Then," Rickey said, "when you go upstairs will you ask Breadon to give me another chance? If he won't, see if you can get him to let Shotton here be the manager."

"O.K.," I said.

"Let me know what Breadon says," Rickey asked.

I went up to Breadon's room. "I came over here to make you the manager," Breadon told me.

"I appreciate that, Mr. Breadon," I said, "but I just don't want to be the manager."

"Well, I don't want Rickey any longer," Breadon said. "I don't want anybody managing my team that won't even come to the games on Sunday, like Rickey."

"You mean Rickey's through?" I asked.

"That's exactly right," Breadon said, "as manager."

"What about Shotton as manager?" I asked.

"I don't want any Rickey man, either," Breadon said.

"Well, I don't want to be manager," I answered.

"Think it over tonight and tell me tomorrow," Breadon said.

I went back down and told Rickey what Breadon had said. Rickey didn't cuss or anything, but he got pretty mad and said he would sell all his stock in the Cardinals. Finally I told Breadon the only way I would be interested in becoming manager would be if I could buy Rickey's stock, which was 1,167 shares and second only to Breadon's. Then baseball could be my business for life.

Rickey still had two years to go on his contract, and became business manager and executive vice-president of the Cardinals. I bought Rickey's stock and became manager for the first time on Memorial Day. We had only one way to go—up. We were in the cellar. I suggested some changes. We strengthened ourselves at catching by getting Bob O'Farrell from the Cubs, and called up shortstop Tommy Thevenow from Syracuse, our farm club in the International League. Managing was new to me and I felt the players really hustled for me. We climbed out of the cellar and finished fourth.

I won the batting championship for the sixth straight year, with a .403 average, led the league in runs batted in (143) and home runs (39).

1926—Even though I had the added responsibilities of manager and led the team from the cellar to fourth place, I didn't get anything extra for managing. My batting average dropped to .317, and some people thought that being player-manager was the reason. I didn't think so. I had gotten the breaks in winning 6 straight championships—averaging .400—and now a few of the breaks went the other way. It was an exciting season. I told the players in spring training that I thought we could win the pennant. We had to patch the team up in spots, and the best thing We did to strengthen ourselves was claim Grover Cleveland Alexander by waivers from the Cubs on June 22 and get Billy Southworth from the Giants for Heinie Mueller. We almost lost the pennant late in September by playing in some exhibition games rather than concentrating on the pennant. Nevertheless, we beat the New York Giants in a double-header on September 28, while the Cincinnati Reds lost. That clinched us the pennant.

All the news wasn't good for me that day. When I got back to the Almanac Hotel to eat supper I had a telegram. My mother had died. I called my aunt and she told me that my mother had heard that we won the pennant

My War with Baseball

and left a message. "Tell Rogers that I don't want anything to interfere with him playing in the World Series." She asked that I play in the series. Needless to say, I was heartbroken. The funeral was delayed until after the Series.

It was a tough series. We played the Yankees, who were managed by Miller Huggins, my first big-league manager. They were big favorites. After we won the World Series I learned that Breadon offered my job to Bill Killefer, one of my coaches, and Killefer turned it down and told me so. I then took a train to Texas for my mother's funeral.

Even though I had managed the Cardinals to their first pennant and World Series in history, Breadon only offered me a one-year contract. I made up my mind that I wasn't going to take anything less than a three-year contract. He definitely had made up his mind that he was only going to sign me for one year.

Something was bound to happen. Still, it was a shock to me when about 8 o'clock on the night of December 20 I got a call from Clarence Lloyd, the Cardinals' traveling secretary. I had been traded to the New York Giants.

The papers called it the biggest trade of all times. The St. Louis fans tried to bring all kinds of pressure on Breadon. Even wrote a letter to the commissioner, Judge Landis, trying to get Breadon to change his mind.

There was a lot more howling. I made a simple statement to the press:

"If they want to trade me, it's all right with me. But it doesn't seem right that I should be traded from a club that I just managed to a world championship. I gave the

Cardinals all I had, and I asked for a three-year contract that I believed I was entitled to. I had always been playing under a three-year contract. I wasn't paid a thing for managing the club—not even a word of congratulations or a complimentary remark. The players weren't even congratulated."

1927—I got the salary I deserved with the Giants. More than I got for managing and playing for the Cards. Thought I'd be cut from under the pressure of managing, but John McGraw, the Giants' manager, told me that when he was away or sick I'd take over. He was a little sick toward the end of the season, and I managed the Giants for a few weeks. It didn't look like I'd get to play for them though, because of the ruling that I couldn't own Cardinal stock and play for another team. Breadon wouldn't offer me what I thought was a fair price, so the league chipped in and added that to Breadon's offer so I could get what was coming to me and could play.

I played in every game that season (155) and had a good year, batting .361—tops for the Giants and 44 points higher than the year I led the Cardinals to the championship. We came in third, a half-game behind the Cardinals.

One night I answered the phone at my home in Chicago. It was long distance.

"This is Judge Fuchs of the Braves," the man on the phone said. "Rogers, I'd be delighted to have you on my team. I just traded for you."

1928—I wasn't the manager of the Braves. Just a player. The Braves didn't do very well, and when you're down in seventh or eighth place, the owner has to make some kind of move. Judge Fuchs asked me to take the

My War with Baseball

manager's job, but I didn't want to see Jack Slattery fired. The only way I would take the job, I told Fuchs, would be if Slattery was definitely going to quit.

Although I wasn't as young as I once was I won my seventh National League batting championship with a .387 average. The Braves came in seventh.

For the third straight year the newspapers carried the headline: HORNSBY TRADED. The deal that sent me to the Cubs for 5 players also involved the most money ($200,000) of any trade in history. The highest-priced one before that was the $137,000 the Yankees paid the Boston Red Sox for Ruth. There were several reasons given in the papers why I was traded, but I suggested the trade to Fuchs so he could have the money to get himself out of debt.

1929—Went to Catalina Island, off Avalon, California, with the Cubs, who were managed by Joe McCarthy. Since the Cubs were the fourth team I was to play for in 4 years, there were several stories saying I was hard to get along with. Some of the writers gave their own opinions, and here's how one Chicago sportswriter described me:

1. He has been one of the first three players to reach the practice field in 10 of the 14 practice sessions since he arrived.
2. He does not kibitz when Manager Joe McCarthy is talking, either on the playing field or in the hotel solarium.
3. Calls all the rookies by their nicknames, high-hatting none.
4. Is the chief Atta-boy shouter in the pepper talk following snappy maneuvers.

5. Chums with none of the established stars, but is friendly to all.
6. Didn't read the papers to find out who won the Derby at Tia Juana last Sunday.

The Cubs had the best group of individual players of any team I ever played on and we won the pennant by 9½ games. We lost to the Philadelphia Athletics in the World Series.

I played in every game (156), hit 40 home runs, batted in 149 runs and had a .380 batting average. I didn't win the batting championship, but I received the National League's Most Valuable Player Award.

1930—Things didn't go as well. I broke my left ankle sliding into third base against the Cardinals in the morning game of a double-header in Wrigley Field late in May. The Cubs didn't win the pennant. They changed managers. They announced it early—on September 25—that I'd be the Cub manager for 1931. So I managed the Cubs against the White Sox in the City Series, and won that for the first time.

1931—Was listed as playing manager, but it didn't look like I'd get to do much playing. I was thirty-five, recovering from a broken leg, and had developed a spur on my heel. On April 24 I knew I wasn't "washed up" by any means. I hit 3 straight home runs against the Pirates. But I treated myself just like another player. I even benched myself for not hitting. I played in 100 games and had a .331 batting average. We came in fourth, and I realized we needed to strengthen ourselves for 1932.

1932—I put together a club that I thought would be capable of winning the pennant. We added Billy Jurges, Billy Herman and Lon Warneke. I wasn't doing much

My War with Baseball

playing—only 19 games—but that wasn't all of my troubles. Bill Veeck, Sr., the president and general manager, tried to make some of my managing decisions from his office and it was obvious we didn't see eye to eye.

I got a message to see him in his office in August. That was the last time I managed the Cubs. Charley Grimm replaced me.

The Cubs went on to win the pennant. I feel I could have won it, too. We were in second place when I was fired, and it wasn't what Grimm did or didn't do that won the pennant for the Cubs. The first-place Pirates, the team to beat, lost 13 straight games.

I didn't even get any share of the World Series money which I was entitled to. Not a penny. (Remember Babe Ruth calling them cheapskates?)

1933—Was now a free agent. Branch Rickey, who now was doing a tremendous job as front-office boss of the Cardinals, hired me as a player and pinch hitter. I hit .335 in 46 games, and at one stretch got 5 straight hits as a pinch hitter. In late July, Bill Killefer had been fired as manager of the Browns and Allen Sothoron had been acting manager. I signed a contract with Phil Ball, owner of the club, to manage the Browns for the remainder of the 1933 season and all of 1934. and 1935.

The Browns were last when I took over, and we finished in the same spot. Later in the winter Mr. Ball died.

1934—We made some good trades and got up to sixth place. I pinch-hit 24 times and got 7 hits for a .304. average.

1935—Was about finished as a player. Pinch-hit 10 times. Several players were sick or injured and we got off to a slow start. The Browns finished seventh, but the club must have been satisfied with my work. On September 17 they signed me to a new three-year contract for the 1936-37-38 seasons.

1936—The Browns finished seventh, which wasn't good, but still was higher than Connie Mack and his Athletics, who slipped to the cellar. I didn't do any playing to speak of—pinch-hit 5 times and got 2 hits, something that used to be just a day's work for me. We might have finished higher, except we were operating under the estate of Mr. Ball and had to sell some players to keep going.

1937—Donald Barnes became the new president of the Browns and picked Bill DeWitt for his general manager. When I was fortunate enough to hit a couple of hot horses and win more than enough money to pay Barnes for the stock in his loan company he had sold me, the fireworks started. It wasn't long afterward, July 21, that DeWitt told me Barnes wanted to see me in his office. He told me I was fired as manager.

It was the middle of the baseball season and there wasn't much demand then for "fired" managers. I wanted to be around baseball, so I played for the Denver Bay Refiners in the National Semipro Tournament. Grover Cleveland Alexander was there, too, with his Springfield, Illinois, team.

1938—Mike Kelly, a friend of mine who owned the Minneapolis team in the American Association, asked me to come to spring training and help out. After that I went to Baltimore of the International League as third-base coach and pinch-hit a few times.

On June 26 Joe Engel, one of the best baseball promoters I know, bought my contract from Baltimore and asked me to manage his Chattanooga Lookouts in the Southern Association for the rest of the year. I did.

1939—Went back to Baltimore as manager of the Orioles.

1940—For the first time since 1915 I didn't have a job in organized baseball in spring training. But I still was around the game. The Rogers Hornsby Baseball School, operating out of Hot Springs, was doing well. In the middle of June I got a call from Jim Humphries of the Oklahoma City team in the Texas League. I took the job as manager, we came in third and made it to the championship game of the play-offs.

1941—Managed Oklahoma City Indians until June 23, when I resigned because the team was short of money. On November 18 I signed a contract to become manager and general manager of the Fort Worth team, which was sort of a home-coming to me. And as general manager and manager I had a license, you might say, to second-guess myself.

1942—The Fort Worth team was in financial trouble, but we at least started the season on even terms when a couple of rich businessmen paid off all the notes. I held my baseball school in Fort Worth before the season started. Fort Worth finished third, which was a big jump. The team had been last the year before. Although I was forty-six years old, I put myself on the active list and on May 4 went up to bat against Houston with the score tied and 2 runners on in the ninth inning. I got a single and we won, 3-1.

My Forty-Eight Years in Baseball

I got some good news in the fall. The club gave me a new contract and I was voted into Baseball's Hall of Fame.

1943—Thought we'd have a good season. But the Texas League directors met to discuss playing during the war years. Fort Worth and Oklahoma City wanted to play, but none of the other clubs did and the league was suspended.

1944—On February 14. I agreed to take Jorge Pasquel's offer to instruct baseball and manage his Vera Cruz team, which played out of Mexico City, in the Mexican League. He was the fellow who made all those $300,000 offers to Ted Williams, Bob Feller, Phil Rizzuto and the big stars, which I contended were just for publicity.

Anyway, I hadn't been around anything like this before. One day I'd have a player on my team. I'd teach him something. Next day he'd use that trick against me—he'd be on another team. Pasquel owned 5 of the teams, and he'd shift the players around because the clubs didn't have contracts for most of their players.

I couldn't speak Mexican and only two players on my team, Chico Hernandez, former Cub catcher, and Chile Gomez, former Phillies infielder, could speak English. So I'd have to give my team pep "talks" by waving my arms and making all kinds of odd gestures.

One day three or four thousand Mexicans pushed against the wall until it fell down. Then they walked into the game free. Another day we beat Puebla, and that night some fans burned down our left-field stands. I don't know why. In fact I didn't know we were supposed to lose so the owner would make more money. I'd had enough. I quit and came back to the United States.

1945—On February 27 I became the director of the Chicago *Daily News'* free baseball school, teaching youngsters all over Illinois and anywhere the *Daily News* was sold, to play baseball.

1946—Taught over 100,000 young boys the strike zone, how to hold their hands to catch a ground ball, and how to hit. I got a lot of satisfaction from this.

1947—Was a personal batting coach for two players—catcher Jim Hegan, outfield Pat Seerey of the Cleveland Indians—during spring training. Then came back to Chicago to continue as director of the baseball school.

1948—Teaching more kids.

1949—Turned announcer, helping do the telecasts of Cub games for WENR-TV in Chicago. Came out of the booth on July 9 for the Old-Timers' Day Game in Wrigley Field.

1950—Was offered a scouting job, but I wanted to wear a baseball uniform again and you can't go scouting in a uniform. Then on February 8 I signed to manage the Beaumont team in the Texas League. Beaumont had a working agreement with the Yankees, but was not a direct-farm club and it hadn't had much success. In fact Beaumont was last, 44 games behind the leader, the year before. We opened the season against San Antonio—a fast kid named Bob Turley pitched against us—and we got off to a slow start. On June 7 we were 19 games out of first place. We were 13½ games out on July 1. We didn't quit. We won the pennant. On September 5 they had Rogers Hornsby Day and gave me a new black

Cadillac. I kept busy during the winter by managing Ponce in the Puerto Rican League.

1951—Replaced Paul Richards as manager of the Seattle Rainiers, who had finished sixth the year before in the Pacific Coast League. We won the pennant and playoffs. And the big-league clubs suddenly became interested in me.

1952—Signed a three-year contract with Bill Veeck to manage the St. Louis Browns, with the complete understanding that he wouldn't mess up the game with clowns and wouldn't tell me how to manage. We got off to a good start and Veeck was doing a helluva job. When we slumped, then Hornsby was doing a terrible job. Then Veeck tried to manage the team and I became a free agent again on June 10.

Gabe Paul, general manager of the Cincinnati Reds, called me and asked me to meet him in Indianapolis. I did, and on July 28 I was named manager of the Reds, succeeding Luke Sewell. We were last then, but came on kind of strong and finished sixth.

1953—We didn't climb any higher in the standings, and when this happens the thing to do is change managers since they get all the blame for losing. On September 17 I was relieved as manager. I wasn't mad at the Reds and I don't think they were mad at me. Then I came back to my home at the Edgewater Beach Hotel in Chicago.

1954—Was named director of Mayor Daley's Youth Foundation Recreation Program, teaching baseball to youngsters. It was a job I really enjoyed.

1955—The year went by fast. Teaching eight- to eleven-year-old kids how to play, and no general managers to tell you how to manage.

1956—No general managers and a lot of fun—running the recreation program.

1957—I loved my job, but I couldn't get big-league baseball out of my blood. The Cubs offered me a job as full-time batting coach. I took it.

1958—I lived just a few minutes away from Wrigley Field, where I'd go every day as Cub coach.

1959—Felt I helped several Cub players with their hitting, working under Bob Scheffing who did a good job bringing the club in fifth. But he was fired and Charley Grimm replaced him.

1960—Grimm didn't want any hitting coach, so I was used as batting instructor for the Cubs' minor-league clubs.

1961—I celebrated my sixty-fifth birthday, which is the age most people retire. I thought about retiring—I didn't need to work—but retiring meant being away from baseball. George Weiss was getting the New York Metropolitans started. He needed a Chicago scout to look over all the major-league players who might appear on the list, or "grab bag," from which he would have to select his team for 1962.

1962—Casey Stengel asked me to be team batting coach for the New York Mets and report to spring training.

How could I say NO?

3. The Game's Not the Same

I'M TIRED of reading stories like "Today's Ballplayers Are Sissies," and "They Don't Play Baseball Any More." Some of them even imply that today's teams couldn't carry old-timers' bats. How do these people—sportswriters or ex-ballplayers—know this? They don't. You can't claim old-time ballplayers and teams are so much better than today's players and teams, any more than you can prove that Boston has prettier girls than Dallas, or that Joe Louis was a better fighter than Jack Dempsey.

Times have changed a helluva lot. Back when I was playing if anybody ever talked about shooting a man up in space with one of those rockets, they'd send for that fellow in the white suit with a strait jacket. When I was managing the St. Louis Cardinals in 1926, people in town thought another young fellow about my age was crazy. This guy, Charles Lindbergh, said he was going to fly an airplane clear across the Atlantic Ocean.

Baseball has changed with the times, believe me. It's as different as the styles of the roaring twenties—spats and flappers and all. Baseball was a scientific game when Ty Cobb, Honus Wagner, Grover Cleveland Alexander and I played. We went after an early lead. If we had a big inning and hit a homer, fine. But we'd try to get on base, steal or bunt to second, then hope we could hit behind the runner for a 1-0 lead. In most cases a good pitcher held the lead.

Today, though, some pitchers—good pitchers, too—can't hold a three- or four-run lead. It's not the pitcher's fault. It's the lively ball and the new style of baseball. Everybody is going for the fences today because that's where the pay-off is. The fans want home runs and the players have to hit them to make big money. Home-run hitters drive Cadillacs. Singles hitters drive Fords. (Ralph Kiner, a home-run slugger with the Pirates, once said on a TV show: "I swing from the end of the bat—that's where the Cadillacs are." And Kiner was appearing on a show sponsored by the Ford Motor Company.)

This home-run craze has everybody worked up. If you were to let the bat boy hit a couple of pitches some day in practice he wouldn't just try to meet the ball. He'd swing right for the fences.

While we used to consider a 1-0 or 2-1 score as a great game, people today would be bored. They crave excitement, not only in baseball, but in everything. People drive faster, and movies and all kinds of shows are sexier.

Sportswriters went wild over the final game of the 1960 World Series between the Pirates and Yankees because there were 5 home runs and the final score was 10-9. Some writers called it the greatest game ever played. It was an exciting game, I grant you, but writers back in the 1920's and 1930's would have given both teams hell

The game's not the same—lighter bats, larger gloves, livelier balls.

My War with Baseball

over the mediocre pitching. People sitting around me at the first game of the 1961 World Series complained it was dull because only two runs were scored in the game. It was a good game.

I would like to have played the scientific game when I managed the Cincinnati Reds in 1952-53. But we didn't have the players for it. We did have, however, Ted Kluszewski, Gus Bell, Jim Greengrass, Wally Post, and Andy Seminick. These fellows hit more home runs in one year than any team until the 1961 Yankees. It was to our advantage to swing for the fences. Besides, we didn't have any pitchers who could hold a 1-0 or 2-1 lead, anyway.

Speaking of Bell, there's a good example of just how players' equipment has changed. Recently somebody got Edd Roush's glove he used to play outfield with for the Reds and New York Giants, and compared it with the glove Bell uses today. (I also know Edd real well, too—played with him on the 1927 Giants team.)

Roush's glove, which is in the trophy case in Baseball's Hall of Fame, measures $8\frac{1}{2}$ inches from the tip of the finger to the end of the glove. It's 8 inches wide. Now Bell's glove is $10\frac{1}{2}$ inches long and $12\frac{1}{2}$ inches wide. Bell says, "I'll make twenty-five catches a year in the webbing of this glove alone. I just stab for the ball and it's in there."

You can't criticize Bell or any other guys for using big gloves which look more like scoops to me. It improves fielding. Everyone today is a big defensive star if he isn't afraid of getting in front of the ball, and of course knows how to use a scoop.

The Game's Not the Same

The lively ball has brought on a need for larger gloves. The ball travels so much faster. Some people have claimed for years that the ball isn't any livelier, but everyone I know who played baseball before the War knows better. And we were proved correct when Roger Maris and Mickey Mantle closed in on Babe Ruth's home-run record during the 1961 season and everybody got all worked up. One of those testing outfits—and a reliable one, too—revealed that today's ball bounces higher, is firmer, and weighs more, even in comparison with the 1953 ball. One test showed that a drive that would have traveled 300 feet 15 years ago would carry 330 feet today.

I scouted the Yankees against the White Sox, September 12, 1961, and Comiskey Park was packed. The fans weren't out to see the White Sox. Everybody wanted to see Maris or Mantle hit a home run. They didn't get any, but Luis Aparicio of the White Sox did. And it was his sixth home run of the season, mind you. The ball had to be livelier. If it wasn't, Aparicio wouldn't be able to hit the ball as far as he could and let it roll, then another time hit it out of the park. And it wasn't but a few days earlier I saw Nellie Fox of the White Sox hit a ball out of the park. They shouldn't be hitting home runs. Fox and Aparicio put together aren't much bigger than Ruth. Anybody can hit homers today with that golf ball—I mean lively ball.

Tris Speaker, who is considered the greatest centerfielder with the glove of all time, used to play just a little way behind the second baseman. All outfielders played shallow—to cut off the singles. Today they back up against the fence for the sluggers and jump straight up in the air at the ball sailing into the stands. If some of these players today were smart they'd hit singles in front of the outfielders playing too far back.

Even bats are different—and should be better. They've been testing them for 100 years and even apple pie was improved after all that testing and experimenting. Today's players swing harder—with much lighter bats. Maris used 33-ounce bats—once a 35-ounce bat—when he hit 61 home runs in 1961. Ruth didn't use anything lighter than 42 ounces when he set the record of 60 home runs.

I'm no expert on making baseball bats, although my bat has been copied more than anyone's. But the Hillerich and Bradsby Company, which makes the Louisville Slugger bats, is. It claims the trend has been to lighter bats. In 1961 it sold mostly 31- and 32-ounce bats. Here's the way Jack McGrath of Hillerich and Bradsby describes the bat situation:

"Today's bats range from thirty-six ounces down to twenty-eight ounces, with Billy Goodman being the only one using the twenty-eight-ounce bat. People like Dick Groat, Ted Kluszewski and Johnny Temple use the thirty-six-ounce bats.

"Babe Ruth once used a bat that weighed as much as fifty-four ounces, and our records show he never ordered anything lighter than thirty-eight ounces. He used mostly forty-two-ounce bats. He was very particular. He selected wood with very tiny knots, not very deep, and the size of a pin. Babe contended that the ball would go harder since the wood around a knot is harder. Most of the sluggers used those wagon tongues.

"Ty Cobb was the first of the big stars to use the narrow handle. The bat he used near the end of his career

The Game's Not the Same

had a handle not much bigger than a Little League bat. Rogers Hornsby had the biggest influence on modern styling. Hornsby realized that the bigger the handle, the less wrist action possible. He used a bat with a little curving handle and big barrel."

Here's Hillerich and Bradsby's table on home runs and bats:

BATTING CHAMPIONS

NATIONAL LEAGUE / AMERICAN LEAGUE

Player	Bat Av.	Bat Weight Ounces	Year	Bat Weight Ounces	Bat. Av.	Player
Larry Doyle	.320	38-44	1915	43	.369	Cobb
Hornsby	.370	37-39	1920	38-40	.407	Sisler
Hornsby	.403	36-39	1925	36-37	.393	Heilmann
Terry	.401	35-39	1930	37	.381	Simmons
Vaughan	.385	35	1935	34	.349	Myer
Garms	.355	34-35	1940	34-35	.352	J. DiMaggio
Cavarretta	.355	32	1945	33-34	.309	Stirnweiss
Musial	.346	32-33	1950	33	.354	Goodman
Ashburn	.338	31-34	1955	31-33	.340	Kaline
Groat	.325	36	1960	32	.320	Runnels

HOME RUN LEADERS

	Home Runs	Ounces		Ounces	Home Runs	
Cravath	24	40-48	1915	44	7	R. Roth
F. Williams	15	38-39	1920	40-47	54	Ruth
Hornsby	35	36-39	1925	38	33	Meusel
Hack Wilson	56	37-38	1930	36-38	49	Ruth
Wally Berger	34	38	1935	35-37	36	Foxx
Mize	43	36	1940	34	41	Greenberg
Holmes	28	34-35	1945	32-33	24	Stephens
Kiner	47	35-36	1950	32-35	37	Rosen
Mays	51	32-34	1955	30-36	37	Mantle
Banks	41	31	1960	31-34	40	Mantle

My War with Baseball

The different type bat and ball has changed the style of pitching altogether. I say that today's pitchers, on the average, can't compare with the pitchers in my time. But again it's not their fault. They could if they were trained correctly. Pitchers, who have to pitch more carefully today to everybody because of this lively ball, start looking to the dugout for help after the fifth or sixth inning. They have been taught to hold on for about this length of time; then a relief pitcher will take care of the rest. I think they could develop pitchers to go 9 innings if they'd try.

Pitchers in my day took more pride in their pitching. They didn't want to come out. Truthfully, we didn't have any relief specialists. If somebody did lose his stuff we'd bring in the best guy we had available. We would, of course, use some judgment and not waste our star pitcher if we were behind 8-2 in the third inning. I hear that Elroy Face and Luis Arroyo can't wait to get into a game as relief pitchers, but they wouldn't have been very popular with the team back in the twenties. We only had 7 or 8 pitchers in my playing days. Today they have 10 or 11.

And today they even train pitchers to be relief pitchers while they're in the minor leagues. Even kids are imitating relief pitchers.

One of the silliest things I've heard in these knocks against present-day players is calling them sissies. One old-time star I knew was quoted in a story: "They don't have tough stars like they used to. Everybody is a sissy. Today a guy runs into somebody else and both of them lay there until they bring out a stretcher. Why Rogers Hornsby, Rabbit Maranville and Ty Cobb were tough enough to operate on themselves."

The Game's Not the Same

Good God!

From What I hear, General Grant, Robert E. Lee and some of those fellows only carried a small first-aid kit and some bandages. But that doesn't mean they were any tougher than General MacArthur just because MacArthur had ambulances behind his troops.

We used to walk two or three miles to school every day and carry our lunch in sirup buckets. Does that mean kids today are lazy or weak because they have school buses and have hot meals at school?

I don't go along with the theory that players get hurt easier today than they did when, say, I managed the 1926 Cardinals or 1932 Cubs or 1953 Reds. There is absolutely no way of telling, and anyone who says players today are brittle is way off base.

There is plenty of truth to the claim that players get better treatment today. In my days a trainer carried aspirin, gauze, iodine; and if anybody got a sore muscle he'd give them a rubdown with liniment. Then use hot towels. We didn't have any whirlpools, pulse takers, muscle vibrators or even X-ray machines. If a player was hurt he and the manager would hold a little conference and decide whether the player should suit up. Or maybe be ready to pinch-hit.

It's entirely different today. They rush guys off to the hospitals for X rays and the trainer says, "Joe Doakes can't play today, tomorrow or the next day. Stiff leg." I certainly don't approve of this—the manager and player should decide who plays. Not the trainer, although most of today's trainers are better than in my playing days.

My War with Baseball

Most trainers in my days got their starts as clubhouse boys cleaning shoes, hanging up uniforms and fixing equipment. Funniest trainer I ever met was Andy Lotshaw of the Cubs. Somebody asked him what he'd do if a player broke a leg.

"That's easy," Andy would say, "call a doctor."

He had a chiropractor's chart in the clubhouse, and if anybody would complain about stiff muscles Andy would look at the chart, then say, "Yep, it's a pelvic nerve." Everything outside of a broken leg was a pelvic nerve.

Andy had his own special "Lotshaw's Liniment." Most times he'd just pour Coca-Cola in his liniment bottle and rub the players down with that. They never knew the difference.

Today Bob Bauman, trainer for the St. Louis Cardinals, is so scientific that he claims there are a bunch of blood vessels all messed up in a pitcher's arm after a hard game. So he puts the pitcher's arm behind his back and massages the fingers like somebody milking a cow. Then he uses ice packs. The most anybody got when I was with the Cards—if he had a stiff arm—was some liniment and the old sun lamp.

Why, Grover Cleveland Alexander, the greatest pitcher of all time, wouldn't let anyone touch his arm. Any time. He even carried his own special brand of liniment. Rub himself down if he wanted a rubdown.

In my days we used to keep injuries quiet so the other team wouldn't hear about them. A publicity man for the New York Yankees made a name for himself a few years ago by keeping a record and boxscore on all the team's injuries. Got lots of ink in the papers.

Just because players did things that seemed "tough" didn't mean they helped themselves any as ballplayers. I've even read of people bragging about some old-time players because they supposedly would grab a couple of bologna sandwiches and a bag of bananas and go on the back of the train and eat. The same fellow criticized today's players because trainers supervised their "balanced diets." I'm no diet specialist, but I'm damn sure that these experienced and educated trainers today know a lot more about a meal than guys who eat out of paper bags and wash it down with beer.

I sure didn't gorge myself with hot dogs, bananas and root beer when I was playing ball. I contended then—and still do—that a player should have steak, salads and milk to be a top-notch player. Or have a decent stomach.

The silly claims about hot dogs and soft drinks have no more to do with a good brand of baseball than the reports that comedy is dead. I admit that the Gashouse Gang, the 1934 Cardinals, was an outstanding team, but those players had the talent and would have been just as great without Pepper Martin and Rip Collins and Dizzy Dean cutting up and telling funny stories.

Actually I contend that some of the players they regard as "characters" from the old days were more stubborn than anything. That's what I thought about Cobb back in 1923, when I played for the Cardinals in a spring-training exhibition against Cobb and the Detroit Tigers in Augusta, Georgia—near where he was raised. In those days it was the practice of the clubs to hire their own umpires to work exhibition games, instead of having them assigned by the league office as they are today. The score was tied. Cobb got a single. He tried to steal second and I tagged him out easily. Cobb raised all kinds of hell with Cy Pfirman, "our" umpire who was working the bases. Steamboat Johnson, the plate umpire, came out to the middle of the field and told Cobb to settle down so we could continue the game. Cobb kept on screaming and waving his arms. He wouldn't move. Johnson warned Ty a couple of times that he would forfeit the game.

Cobb didn't move either—and the umpire forfeited the game to us. The clubs had to refund the money, and there were 5,000 or 6,000 people in the stands, too.

We all went back to the hotel and got dressed. Cobb, though, was still following the umpires around and yelling. An hour or so later, after he finally cooled off, he came down where we all were and asked us to come back and finish the game. Wouldn't have done any good. Everybody had got their money back and left.

Later, Judge Landis fined Cobb's team the amount we lost, since we split the gate 50-50.

Cobb, Babe Ruth, Rabbit Maranville and some of the other "characters" always got their way like this. I have nothing against any of them, but this kind of attitude wouldn't be tolerated today.

Now what I consider comedy isn't really dead, although it might as well be for all I'm concerned. Casey Stengel pulled the funniest stunt I ever saw. I was playing for the Cardinals, and Casey was playing for the Brooklyn Dodgers. He did something to attract the crowd's attention so they would start riding him when he came to bat. Then he tipped his cap, and a sparrow flew out from under it. People still do things like that. Jimmy

Piersall, a great competitor, takes a swing at a butterfly every now and then. Or throws a few things in the other team's dugout. That's comedy, isn't it?

If today's games seem dull, it isn't a lack of comedy. A person who used to watch baseball games played in an hour and a half is bored with today's two- and three-hour games. But still that doesn't mean the play isn't as good. Wouldn't matter if the games were four hours long.

Back when Alexander, for example, pitched a game in exactly 59 minutes, a manager didn't change pitchers and bring in a right-hander to face a right-handed hitter, then switch and play the percentages of using a left-hander. In tight games some managers switch pitchers two or three times an inning to face batters who are hitting on the same side of the plate. They have to stall to warm up pitchers. They have to do more managing today.

While Chuck Dressen was managing the Dodgers, he had an unusual experience when he was stalling. His starting pitcher suddenly blew up and Dressen didn't have time to warm up Clyde King, his best relief pitcher. The other team loaded the bases in 3 or 4 pitches by King.

So Dressen went out and told Pee Wee Reese, the shortstop and captain, to call time and pretend there was something in his eye so King could throw some more warm-up pitches. Pee Wee put on his little act. Infielders Jackie Robinson and Billy Cox tried to help him get the "speck" out of his eye.

But instead of King throwing to Roy Campanella, the catcher, he went out to see if he could help Reese.

My War with Baseball

One thing that is uncalled for and delays the game for at least 10 minutes is dragging the infield. We didn't drag the infield in my days and everybody did O.K. But today it's as certain as the Star-Spangled Banner. Now in my opinion they don't drag that infield especially to smooth out any little rough spots. They're just trying to get the people to leave their seats and buy more beer—buy anything. They sell a lot more things at the park now, and I understand that concession profits are almost double what they were in the days when I played. Which is all right if they want to get every nickel they can.

Night baseball has caused a lot of changes, too. Players, on the average, don't stay in the majors as long as they used to. I played 23½ years, and 20-year men were common. About the only 20-year players lately have been Early Wynn, Ted Williams, Stan Musial and Enos Slaughter. Night ball, and not a player's guts, is responsible for that.

Baseball was always been meant to be a daylight game, but we're going to continue to have night baseball as long as people want to make money. And the minor leagues, what few of them are left, wouldn't even be operating if it weren't for the lights.

I can't say that night baseball is harmful statistics-wise to all players. I've had players I managed with the St. Louis Browns and Cincinnati Reds claim they could hit better at night. Statistics proved it, too. Night ball helps many pitchers a lot. Especially those who have a great deal of sharp breaking stuff. Or can keep the ball low.

Just the same, no matter how good the lights are they throw things out of proportion. Certain outfielders can't get the jump on the ball as good at night. Most hitters can't see as well. It upsets routine. Say a team plays an extra-inning night game, the players might not get to sleep before 2 or 2:30 in the morning. A player needs at least 8 hours' sleep to play decent ball the next day. I always got 10 to 11 hours. So this player has to be up at 9:30 to eat breakfast for an afternoon game. Players cool off much faster at night, and that isn't good for the muscles.

Players today are just as fast as in my day—and before. Ty Cobb, who in my opinion is the greatest player of all time, still holds the stolen-base record of 96 he set in 1915; the year I came to the major leagues. To hear people talk about Ty today, he would steal 200 bases. He wouldn't come close to stealing 96. Or 66. Not that he wasn't a great base runner. But the idea was to get on base and—if it was a good base runner like Cobb, Max Carey or Edd Roush—to try to steal second instead of sacrifice. They don't play Cobb's way anymore. Actually, Luis Aparicio of the Chicago White Sox might be just as fast as many old-timers.

One of the excuses people use in building up Cobb to steal 200 bases today is the lack of good catchers. Well, for their information, 99 percent of the bases stolen are stolen off the pitcher—not the catcher. Cobb or Aparicio studied the moves and habits of pitchers—they'd catch a pitcher making a slight error, then take off.

Just because there aren't as many people in the stands as 20 years ago doesn't mean that baseball is dying. Or that people don't care. When I played or managed against the Dodgers in the twenties and thirties, there never were less than 12,000 to 15,000 people in the stands at any time. Right after I took over the Cincinnati

My War with Baseball

Reds in 1952 we went to Brooklyn and I was sort of stunned. Only 4,000 or 5,000 people at the game.

I asked Harold Parrot, the traveling secretary of the Dodgers, what happened to his crowds.

"Rog," he said, pointing to three or four television cameras, "there's our crowds. Seven hundred and fifty thousand dollars a year."

I'd say that more people see big-league baseball today than ever before. On TV, of course.

Even if there wasn't any television the attendance decline—it's down everywhere—doesn't mean baseball isn't as interesting or people don't care anymore.

When I played, the only entertainment for players was movies or baseball or a speakeasy if you could sneak in one. Today they have fancy air-conditioned bars on every corner—TV, of course; more golf courses, tennis courts, all kinds of boats and fishing equipment; more cars. And there are other professional sports. There wasn't much interest in pro football a few years ago.

The thing that people don't consider is the new expressways. It used to be a major trip to fight the traffic out of town to go fishing, hunting, boating or even visiting kinfolk. Now they can get on an expressway and they're out there just about as quickly as they can go to the ball park and find a place to park.

I do think, though, that baseball has been foolish in televising into minor-league towns. There used to be a rule that barred the big leagues from even broadcasting its games into a city that had a club in professional baseball. The Department of Justice made the major leagues repeal this rule because it was afraid of an injunction. So they flooded every town with fancy radio broadcasts and TV. Messed up everything.

Baseball hasn't helped itself either, by expanding to 10 teams in each league. Especially in these days of tough competition for fans. In the long run, a 10-team league is certain to hurt interest. Who can get excited about teams that are fifth, sixth, seventh, eighth, ninth and tenth in the standing? It was hard enough with an 8-team league.

It would have been much smarter, in my opinion, if baseball had expanded to three 8-team leagues. The American League was off base in expanding to 10 teams just on the spur of the moment by putting another team in Los Angeles and switching franchises around to get a team in St. Paul-Minneapolis. I grant you Minnesota deserved a big-league team. They didn't have to rush out to Los Angeles like they discovered more gold. Los Angeles waited 90 years for its first big-league team, and I don't think the folks there were going to beat down the doors if they had to wait another year or so for their second team.

Getting back to players, their attitudes today have changed, but they try just as hard as in my playing days. Oh, the ones who get the big bonuses don't have as much incentive, but on the average the players want to make good. I know from experience as batting coach for the Chicago Cubs in 1957-59 that all players are tickled to death to have an experienced coach give them good advice. Especially hitting. Everybody loves to hit.

When I came up to the majors in 1915 there weren't any coaches around to teach hitting. Let alone fool with rookies like me. I learned all my baseball by listening and

My War with Baseball

watching older players; and by sitting around hotel lobbies and taking to Miller Huggins, my first big-league manager; and by getting somebody to pitch to me after the rest of the team had gone in. So players today should develop quicker than old-timers. Besides that, most of them are starting out in the kid leagues.

Some clubs have been criticized for having specialized training. Like having a track coach to teach some players how to get a quick start. We didn't even think of hiring anybody like that in my days, but I'm convinced that if you are going to hire a man to teach players to run fast you should get somebody like a track coach who knows something about it. It sure can't hurt anything.

I contend every manager should have a special batting coach. There have been some poor hitters who became good managers. So what business does a .220 hitter—Leo Durocher or Charley Dressen—have trying to tell people how to hit? They know how to manage, I grant you. Same thing at Cincinnati, where manager Fred Hutchinson won the pennant. He was a pitcher, and no pitcher ever knew how to hit very good. Except Babe Ruth.

Now that's one comparison that really boiled me. When I took over the St. Louis Browns as manager in 1952, they were the worst team in big-league baseball. But I got those guys in shape. We won a lot of early-season games and we were right up in the pennant race for a month or so. They claimed I was a slave driver in spring training. I had specialized training. Many clubs have two workouts a day. But I only had one, which lasted from 2½ to 3 hours. But we worked on baseball. We didn't just hit a couple of balls, then sit around talking about the game. When we weren't hitting, fielding or throwing

The Game's Not the Same

we were running or doing something to improve ourselves.

I grant you that today's spring trainings are too long. They could be shortened by three weeks and accomplish just as much. But times have changed in this, too. You'd get fined in my days for taking a wife and family to spring training. Today the whole family goes down, which I don't think is good. This isn't a vacation in the sun. Or a time to take the kids to the beach and hunt nice little shells. Besides, some families argue, and this doesn't help a guy get into shape to play big-league baseball.

Today's players do, of course, have many more things on their minds. They plan more for the time when they're finished in baseball. They run bowling alleys, become stockbrokers—things like that. Whitey Ford could quit baseball tomorrow and be a stockbroker the next day. Many of them even read that *Wall Street Journal*. In my days we'd never heard of it.

When I was in my prime I didn't even consider an off-season job. Baseball was my life, and I was making a good living. So why should I? I maintained—and still do to some extent—that a player must get all the rest he can. He plays seven hard months—or should, anyway. Anybody has only a certain amount of energy to burn up. A guy who goes wild and throws his training routine out the window in the wintertime, even if it's necessary in his off-season job, is voluntarily shortening his playing career. After I became a regular I rested, went quail and duck hunting around Illinois and Missouri, and occasionally went deer hunting in my home state of Texas. Most players who were making good money and didn't have to get a winter job to tide them over to spring usually bought farms and ranches and rested up, too.

My War with Baseball

Although there's been a lot of publicity on some of the Yankees getting caught after hours in the Copacabana in New York, I seriously doubt that today's players are any wilder or bigger playboys than in my days. Lots of players on teams I was on went to those outdoor beer gardens and speakeasies. I never went along with them, because I didn't drink and didn't know how to dance and just would have been a wet blanket on some probably pretty good parties. I'd usually go back to the hotel, eat supper, then get rested up for the next day's game. But I didn't see anything wrong with what they were doing, as long as they didn't overdo it and disgrace the baseball uniform.

You don't have to be unreasonable on a player's night life—old days or modern times. When I managed I let my players set their own curfews. If anyone wanted to stay out late for some special reason, all he had to do was ask me. If the club owner, general manager or a sportswriter called me at 2 or 2:30 in the morning and said two of my star players were in the cocktail lounge downstairs with a couple of sharp-looking blondes, I wanted to say, "Yes, I know. It's so-and-so's anniversary and I gave him permission to stay up late with his wife."

Now getting back to when I was playing. When we made a mistake that cost us a game, or we were in a slump, we'd sit around the clubhouse for half an hour or more and discuss ways to improve ourselves. Players don't do too much of that today, because they have other interests. Baseball was all we knew. When John McGraw called a meeting, though, there wasn't anything voluntary. He'd raise all kinds of hell. Bawl the team out for two or three hours.

The Game's Not the Same

Of course I can see why some people insist they don't play ball like they used to. It's only human nature for me to think that nobody today could touch the 1926 Cardinals. I'm sure that just about every manager who has won a World Series feels the same way.

I'm certain in my mind that no team today could touch the 1921-23 New York Yankees and the 1917-20 Chicago White Sox. But don't bet on it.

4. There Won't Be Any More .400 Hitters

Rogers Hornsby, St. Louis Cardinals	.424	1924
Nap Lajoie, Philadelphia Athletics	.422	1901
Ty Cobb, Detroit Tigers	.420	1911
George Sisler, St. Louis Browns	.420	1922
Ty Cobb, Detroit Tigers	.410	1912
Joe Jackson, Cleveland Indians	.408	1911
George Sisler, St. Louis Browns	.407	1920
Ted Williams, Boston Red Sox	.406	1941
Harry Heilmann, Detroit Tigers	.403	1923
Rogers Hornsby, St. Louis Cardinals	.403	1925
Ty Cobb, Detroit Tigers	.401	1922
Rogers Hornsby, St. Louis Cardinals	.401	1922
Bill Terry, New York Giants	.401	1930

This is a list of everybody who has batted over .400 in the big leagues in what's called modern times. I suggest they fix it up on a nice bronze sign. It's a permanent list. There won't be any more .400 hitters—ever.

When you swing wild—and swing from the heels—your batting average naturally drops. This is why guys are winning the league batting championships with averages like .320 and .325. In my playing days you had trouble breaking into the top 5 with averages like those. Again, I'm not knocking today's players. But I understand people asking why, if baseball is as good as it was 30 years ago, the batting averages aren't as high.

Well, to tell you the truth nobody cares about batting averages any more. All they care about is home runs. And they're a helluva lot easier to hit today than any time before. When I managed the Reds in 1952-53 I heard of this experience on home runs which I feel is the typical feeling throughout baseball. One National League player's batting average had dropped to something like .235. So the coach, a guy from the old school like me, suggested that he just try to meet the ball rather than swing wild for the fences. He did and got 11 hits in the next 28 times at bat; which is batting at a nice .393 rate. His last hit was a home run. And that homer did it.

The next day the player was swinging with all his might. He got a measly 2 hits in the next 19 times at bat. The coach chewed the player out and wanted to know why he went back to swinging for the fences.

"Well," the player said, "nobody paid any attention to me when I hit singles. But the newspapers gave me a headline off that last homer. They pay off on home runs and headlines and I want to get big money in this business."

The front office and not the players are to blame for this long-ball attitude. When a player goes in to sign a contract the man in charge doesn't say, "How many base hits did you get; how many times did you get on base; and how many times did you score or knock somebody in? " It's "How many home runs did you hit?"

Or the man gets up and goes into another room where they keep the big scrapbook. They look through it to see how many headlines the player got. The headlines aren't

There Won't Be Any More .400 Hitters

about the player who gets 3 or 4 singles or drives in 2 or 3 runs. The big print says: SO-AND-SO WINS. SO-AND-SO HITS HOMER.

It's only human nature for any ambitious American playing baseball to try to do something where he can make the most money. Everybody is all excited over the homer—and will be even more so now after Roger Maris' and Mickey Mantle's hitting sprees—and swing as hard as they can. That's where they're all wrong.

You don't have to swing hard to hit a home run. *I never tried to hit a home run in the 23½ years I played in the big leagues.* Not once. The records show I hit 302 home runs and led the National League in homers for two seasons—with 42 in 1922, and 39 in 1925. I didn't let the home runs excite me enough to swing wild. I had a batting average of over .400 in both of those seasons.

I never knew when I hit a home run! I just tried to meet the ball, and didn't try to get fancy. I tried to hit the ball in the largest safe area—straight up the middle of the diamond. The pitcher was my target. I would have liked to hit him each time. Today the home-run-happy guys pick out somebody in the bleachers or the flagpole as their targets. And of course I tried to let all the bad balls go by. There have been some outstanding hitters in the major leagues in recent years who've ruined themselves by swinging at about everything they pitch.

Batting slumps, or most of them today, are caused by guys losing their heads over home runs.

Now there's no sense trying to fool everybody into thinking that every hitter in my days was a superman. They turned on the lights in the ball parks in 1935, which was just about the time my playing career was over, and

Home Run Champ 1918

There Won't Be Any More .400 Hitters

The only reason for not saying it, is that you might have a lot of stock in the light-bulb companies. While some hitters claim they like to hit at night, it's pretty hard to follow a pitch under the waistline. The biggest problem of hitting today is adjusting to conditions at night, then going to daylight and back to night. There are all kinds of reflections to worry about, too. By the time some hitters learn to adjust they're too old to play ball.

While the lights have cut the averages some, they're not enough handicap alone to keep a top hitter from batting .400. Ted Williams did it in 1941. When he was thirty-nine years old and had a bum leg he hit .388, and if he had got 5 or 6 more hits he would have batted over .400. That was just back in 1957. Ted didn't go insane over homers, and while he had a good average in the big leagues he was always pretty close to the top in the home-run race. In all fairness, though, the Red Sox didn't play as many night games as the other clubs.

The livelier ball helps guys to hit more homers today. And it's much easier to hit a home run because all the parks have been chopped down to put in more seats. We'll use Yankee Stadium for an example, since that's where Babe Ruth played when he hit his 60 home runs in 1927 and where Roger Maris and Mickey Mantle play. The right-field section, where Ruth, Maris and Mantle hit most of their home runs, was shortened 30 feet in 1930 when they built an extension on the stands.

They've shortened the right center and center sections of other parks in the American League, too. Washington's Griffith Stadium is now 25 feet closer; Boston's Fenway Park is 45 feet shorter; Chicago's Comiskey Park is 25 feet shorter; Cleveland's Municipal Stadium is 60 feet shorter; Detroit's Tiger Stadium is 25 feet shorter;

and Kansas City's park is 45 feet closer than the park owned by the Philadelphia Athletics, the team they replaced. The Baltimore Orioles, who used to be the St. Louis Browns, have a park 25 feet shorter than the park in St. Louis. And Ruth didn't get to play against the new Los Angeles Angels, who have a park that's only 345 feet to left center and right center, where most home runs are hit.

There's the National League, too, where I did my playing. I didn't get to play in the Dodgers' old park—the Los Angeles Coliseum—where the left-field screen is only 251 feet. You could throw balls over that.

All you have to do is look at the list of home-run leaders to see for yourself how the homer has been easier to hit just about every year. Ever heard of Clifford Clarence Cravath, who played for the Red Sox, White Sox and Senators, and went down to Minneapolis when it was in the American Association? He finally made good with the Philadelphia Phillies. He was a big, lumbering outfielder—weighed over 200 pounds—and had nicknames like Gavvy, Cactus, and Wooden Shoes. Chances are you haven't heard of him. Well, he held the big-league record of 24 home runs in one year until Babe Ruth hit 29.

When I came to the big leagues in the last part of the 1915 season, Cravath was getting as much publicity as Maris and Mantle do today. He led the Phillies to the National League pennant and was the game's greatest home-run slugger. A right-handed hitter—they called his bat a "fence post"—he won the home-run title 5 times and tied another time. The most he ever hit in one year was 24. He played in Baker Bowl, the smallest park in the major leagues, and people said that was the reason he hit such a sensational number of home runs. He won

There Won't Be Any More .400 Hitters

the 1918 championship with 8 home runs. Eight is correct. That's not one of those typographical error things, either. He beat me out—I hit 5 home runs in 115 games. I hit 8 home runs myself in 1920, but Gavvy, who was also the manager of the Phillies, won the championship with 12.

The same thing was going on over in the American League. In 1915 Bob Roth, who played for the White Sox and Indians, won the league championship with 7. Walter Pipp of the Yankees won it with 12 homers in 1916, and 9 in 1917. The next year, 1918, Babe Ruth, who was a pitcher and outfielder for the Red Sox, tied for the American League with 11 home runs.

Now, I've heard talk that this is when they started changing the ball a little to make the game more exciting and overcome some of the bad publicity caused by the 1919 White Sox, who were involved in the World Series fix and became known as the Black Sox. Home runs really became popular in the American League. Babe Ruth, who was then playing for the Yankees, hit 54 home runs.

I don't think they got the new ball over to the National League right away. Fred (Cy) Williams of the Phillies, who was also playing in that little park, won the league championship with 15. The following year (1921) Ruth hit 59 homers, and George Kelly of the New York Giants hit 23 to win in the National League.

In 1922 Kenneth Williams of the St. Louis Browns led the American League with 39 home runs. He used a 54-ounce bat. St. Louis had both leaders that year. I was playing for the St. Louis Cardinals and won the National League with 42. [Editor's note: Blunt-talking but modest Hornsby also led the league in batting with a .401

My War with Baseball

average, runs batted in with 152, doubles with 46, hits with 250 and runs with 141.]

People have been in love with home runs ever since. The owners know they have to satisfy the fans to make money, and people have started to care less every year about singles and doubles hitters. I know that the manufacturers of baseballs claim indignantly that not a single thing has been changed in the ball since 1923. It's still made of cork center, 100 percent wool yarn, and a hand-stitched horsehide cover. That's what you'd expect them to say. If I had been making blankets for 100 years, I wouldn't say out loud that they're not as warm as they used to be, either. This home-run ball has replaced the batting averages.

Most men who have batted over .400 in the major leagues don't agree with me that there won't be another .400 hitter. Ty Cobb, who was the only man besides myself to bat over .400 in 3 different years, made it clear right before he died in the summer of 1961. "I just know that somebody," Ty said, "will come along and hit four hundred. I don't know who it will be, but somebody will do it. It can be done. Mark my words."

Sure it can be done. But they're going to have to find somebody besides these guys in the big leagues today. It will have to be done by somebody who hasn't heard of the home run.

Cobb was just about the smartest hitter you'll ever want to see at the plate. He could move in and crowd the plate if he thought the pitcher was going to give him a curve. A left-handed batter, Cobb made a science out of hitting. He was liable to hit from 3 or 4 different places in the box, all during one turn at bat. He never hit more

There Won't Be Any More .400 Hitters

than 12 home runs in one year, and won the 1909 championship with 9, but his lifetime batting of .367 is the highest in history. Now I don't suggest Cobb's tricks to any young hitters today. It's tough enough to learn one good stance.

Back to .400 hitters. Ted Williams, a .406 hitter in 1941, goes out on the limb and says flatly, "Hell, yes, there'll be more four-hundred hitters. I hit three-eighty-eight in fifty-seven and could have hit four hundred if I hadn't had all that trouble with my legs."

Ted Williams, I grant you, is very capable of hitting .400. But there just aren't any more Williamses around. Williams, Stan Musial and Joe DiMaggio were the only great hitters in the big leagues in the last 20 years I can truthfully call great. Ted and Joe have retired and Stan's way past his prime. Still, no matter how good they are they don't compare with Cobb, Ruth and Speaker, my all-time outfield. Joe Jackson certainly belongs on any all-time hitting team, but is almost always left off because his name was mentioned with the White Sox World Series scandal.

Williams has said that Mantle, Willie Mays and maybe Hank Aaron have a chance to hit .400, and if anybody does it one of these three will. Mays is probably the best hitter in the big leagues, in my opinion. But he goes after too many bad pitches to ever hit close to .400. So he'll never do it, although he has the ability.

Mantle has an advantage over Mays. He has as much power and can hit from both sides of the plate. His power also makes the outfield back up more and leaves a lot of places open for him to hit singles. But he's always taped up or has his knees wrapped up, and I don't think he's quite tough enough to do it. He couldn't even play in the first two World Series games.

Mantle has much more power than Maris. Maris, who is a left-handed hitter, is strictly a right-field pull hitter and has the advantage of the short right-field line in Yankee Stadium. They didn't pitch him very smart in 1961. Threw him too many inside pitches, which is all he's looking for so he can pull the ball. He'll never have a big average. Let alone .400. He couldn't hit .400 if he added all his averages together.

No matter how many home runs Maris goes on to hit I still don't think he can ever compare with Ruth. Babe had a lifetime batting average of .342. And they pitched more carefully to Ruth than they do to Maris. Look at the walks to Maris and Ruth if you don't believe me. They gave Ruth their first 2 pitches way inside, hoping he'd pull the ball foul. Then they'd give him outside pitches, which isn't, of course, where he liked to hit. I maintain strongly that Ruth could have hit .400 if he wanted. He was a big guy who concentrated on home runs. But he still had averages of .393 and .378 with that last average winning him the American League batting championship in 1924. He batted .356 the year he hit those 60 home runs.

What'd Maris hit?

Bill Terry, who hit .401 for the Giants in 1930, also doubts that there will be another .400 hitter. He does think, however, that Mantle would have a good chance to do it "if he used some hitting sense."

True. But it's too late in his career for him to try to hit instead of pulling the ball. After the 1961 season he'll never try just for average. He's been drawing home-run pay and he's not about to give that up for singles' money. He's seen those singles hitters driving those cheap little cars so they can get more miles to the gallon of gas.

George Sisler, who hit .420 for the St. Louis Browns the same year I hit .401 for the St. Louis Cardinals, says somebody will hit .400 again. "There's not any reason for it not being done," George says, "especially if they'd quit this guess hitting. Guess hitting is terrible. You know, guys guessing it's going to be a curve, slider and so forth before they ever throw the ball, then swinging those little bats as hard as they can. They should get a decent bat and swing just to meet the ball." George used a 42-ounce bat, which is about 10 ounces heavier than most batters swing today. Did all right, too. Averaged .340 in 16 big-league seasons.

Again, in defense of today's players, not all of them ever get the chance to be great hitters. Two-platooning has caused that. This makes a more exciting game, I know, but I figure the two-platoon was meant for football and I don't know much about football. We used to pick out the best players, and that was your line-up until somebody got hurt. Or a regular loafed or went bad and there was somebody on the bench who was better. You almost need a special coach to keep account of all the players who have been in many games.

Now of course if you're leading in the late innings and some guy who couldn't outrun a possum is playing right field, it's not dumb to take him out for a better defensive man. But today when they bring kids up to the big league they just let the right-handers hit against left-handed pitchers and the left-handed batters hit against right-handed pitchers. Using that two-platoon to do that. You can't develop a good hitter that way. If the kid has ability you've got to let him hit against both right-handers and left-handers. Pro baseball wasn't meant to be a specialist's game—like football where they have offensive and defensive teams. This ruins a lot of young players. I remember a big-league club filling the bases in the first inning of the opening game of the season recently. This brought up a rookie who had been the hottest thing in Florida during spring training. What's the manager do? Takes the kid out for a pinch hitter! What in the world do you think that did to the boy's spirit? Or confidence? Probably killed it.

Too many managers are overmanaging. Games are won in the seventh, eighth, and ninth innings, so I'll grant you there is some excuse for managers switching all around in the late innings. But not in the early innings, unless the pitcher is getting clobbered.

We had two-platooning in my days, but not much. George Stallings started it with the 1914 Boston Braves. He had a right-handed hitter named Mann who couldn't hit right-handers but murdered left-handers. So he didn't play him against right-handers. Branch Rickey did some platooning with the St. Louis Browns. But neither of them thought it would lead to the present-day system.

You can't blame Casey Stengel for platooning. He had one of the best-equipped teams in history when he managed the Yankees. He never took too many chances or hurt the team by any switching around. He had better players on the bench than some teams had playing smart baseball. Paul Richards, though, wound up one day with the pitcher playing third base.

I feel that the additional two teams in each league will end some of the platooning. The guys on the bench won't be quite as good as in the past—they'll be playing first string for other teams—and the manager will be hurting the team to platoon in many instances.

In all the craze for the long ball, good sacrifice bunting has become as scarce as beer trucks at the W.C.T.U. conventions they hold not too far from where I live on Chicago's North Side. Why, when Fred Haney became the general manager of the new Los Angeles Angels team he studied the list of players he had to draft his team from to get started in 1961 and really looked puzzled. "Why," Fred said, "there's not a man on this list who can bunt. Not one."

There aren't many men on all the other teams put together who can bunt. It's not hard. All you have to do is take some good advice and practice a little. I didn't have any trouble teaching good bunting when I was working as a coach in 1953-56. I was instructing eight- to eleven-year-old kids in Mayor Daley's Youth Foundation Program in Chicago, too, mind you. Little kids wearing Davy Crockett T-shirts. Some grown men playing pro baseball don't want to learn to sacrifice, because a sacrifice is just what the word means—sacrifice your time at bat to advance a runner from either first to second, or second to third. But they don't want to give up a chance to hit a home run!

Even the few people who try to bunt do it entirely wrong. Don't even know the fundamentals. They hold the bat too damn tight. Here's how simple it is to sacrifice-bunt. Hold your rear hand loose on the bat, and your first finger and thumb of your lead hand just below the trademark of the bat. Don't fool around with a lot of fancy stuff before you meet the ball, like running and bunting. When you see the pitch coming bring your rear leg around and face the pitcher. Hold the bat perfectly still and loose. Until you come in contact with the ball. Do this six inches or more in front of the plate. The looseness of the bat deadens the ball and makes it roll slow enough to give the guy you're trying to advance time to get to the next base before the fielder can make the play.

Simple, isn't it? Several hundred big leaguers can't do it. Even pitchers, who are normally, of course, lousy hitters, don't even try to learn how to sacrifice. No, they go up to the plate swinging from their heels, hoping they'll hit a home run sometime, too, before their career is over. Or they'll bunt a high pitch straight up in the air.

During my playing days (I have a batting average of .403 from 1921 to 1925 when I batted .397, .401, .384, .424, and .403) players used to hit .385 and sometimes better and never win the championship. They hit like I did—not trying to kill the ball, and most important, being ready to hit at all times.

I maintain a player should take a natural stance. Stand where it is most comfortable to you. I originally stood in the middle of the box, close to the plate. Later on I found this wasn't the best way for me. I stood as far back in the box as the law allowed, figuring I'd have more time to see the pitch break or come over the plate. You don't have to experiment during a game. Take a little time after the game—you don't have to race anybody away from the park—or show up a little early and work on things like that. When you first step into the box, swing your bat or lay it on your shoulder—whichever feels most natural to you. But have the bat ready when the pitcher lets go of the ball so you won't have to make any false moves that hurt your timing. Timing is 50 percent of hitting.

There Won't Be Any More .400 Hitters

Have your arms away from the body. When your bat is in hitting position your weight shifts to your rear leg. The front foot then becomes a pivot foot. Never hit off the fore foot. Never lift your rear foot off the ground.

You get your power off your rear leg, your arms and the follow-through.

Learn the strike zone, which is between the batter's armpits and his knees and is 17 inches wide. Most of the time you're not going to get anything by hitting pitches outside the strike zone. If a ball is in the strike zone you can hit one pitch as well as another. Doesn't make any difference if it's a fast ball, change-up, curve or slider. Just swing level and stride into the pitch. Just try to hit the ball through the middle of the diamond. If you do it right the home runs will take care of themselves.

If more guys don't start trying to hit this way and quit being so home-run happy somebody will be able to write a story in a few years called "Will There Ever Be Another .300 Hitter?"

5. The General Problem—General Managers

WHEN I was managing the Chicago Cubs in 1932 we were trailing the Boston Braves by 3 runs in the last of the eleventh inning in the first game of a Sunday doubleheader. Frank House was pitching for the Braves. We had the bases full. I decided to put the best hitter I had available in to pinch-hit for catcher Rollie Hemsley. So I grabbed a bat and went up to the plate.

Hemsley was very popular with Cub fans, and I got a loud razzing from the crowd. I worked House to the full 3 and 2 count and knew he had to come in with the pitch. I was lucky enough to hit it in the right-field bleachers for a home run and we won the game. The fans threw their straw hats on the field. To this day I consider this just about the best move I ever made.

When I got back to the dugout, however, somebody said that Bill Veeck, Sr., the general manager and president of the Cubs, wanted to see me in his office. He had the riot act ready.

"Say, I want to know one thing," Veeck said. "Why did you put yourself on a spot like that?"

"On a spot?" I said. "I don't know what you mean."

For a manager to hold his job today he has to "yes" the general manager.

The General Problem—General Managers

"Well, why did you go up there and bat for Hemsley?" he said.

"I thought I was the best hitter," I answered. "In fact, I'm a damn sight better hitter than him any day."

"Suppose you'd struck out? " he said sarcastically.

"Well, what the hell," I popped right back, "it wouldn't have been the first time. I've struck out a lot of times with the bases loaded."

"Yeah, I know all that," Veeck said, "but look at the position it put you in. Really on the spot in front of all those people."

"I didn't consider it any spot," I said. "I don't manage scared. I play the best man I can possibly get in the best spot."

"Well, now," Veeck said, "that's O.K. but just don't do it again."

"Mr. Veeck, as long as I'm manager of the club," I answered real sharp, "I'm going to use the best man at the time I think I should."

And I did.

And I didn't manage the Cubs too much longer.

And I don't have a big-league managing job today, either.

That incident with Mr. Veeck, who is the father of the Bill Veeck who thinks major league baseball is a Halloween party, took place 30 years ago, but goes to show how general managers also like to be field managers. Conditions are even worse today. For a manager to hold his job today he has to "yes" the general manager, which is something I will never do and is one of the main reasons I don't have a big baseball job. Some general managers even barge into the clubhouse and tell the players what to do.

It's not the people who are general managers that I don't like. It's the system. And I'm not saying all general managers are bad. There are some very good ones, just like there are good and bad players. Not very many good ones, though. Today's general managers make the manager cooperate with them on his line-up. And any time the manager doesn't do exactly what the general manager orders, the general manager tells the owner or president of the club that their manager is a "lemon" and insists that they get rid of him. And uses the manager as his alibi.

How many times have you seen managers given the credit in the newspapers today for making a good trade? Very seldom. The general manager, I guarantee you, assures everyone that he made the trade. But if the trade doesn't pan out, his alibi to the owner (and usually the newspaper guys) is simple: "I got him the players, but he just can't win. We'll have to get a new manager to save the ball club."

Many times the general manager doesn't even consult the manager before he makes a trade. It would be nice, I think, if he asked the manager what positions he thought the team needed to improve. The only thing most general managers worry about is looking good. Even if they ask the manager they don't pay any attention to him.

Many managers don't even pick the starting line-up today. The general manager tells the field manager—the guy who is supposed to be running the team—who to use.

The General Problem—General Managers

He'll say, "Play so-and-so at second base." It's obvious why. He personally traded for so-and-so, while the previous general manager had traded for the other second baseman. It doesn't make the new general manager look good to have the other second baseman outplay his man.

I'm not trying to claim everything the general manager does is wrong and everything the field manager does is right. But they are completely separate jobs and they should be kept that way.

The general or business manager's job originally was—and still is as far as I'm concerned—supervising everything but the players and handling all the paper work. He is hired to make the best deal he can on television and radio rights; to supervise the upkeep of the ball park, and determine where repairs are needed; to represent the club on policy matters at all the league meetings; to hire people to work at other jobs around the park; to check on ticket sales and do things—like make speeches if he has time—to boost the ticket sales if the club is playing only so-so.

The general manager is usually more educated in these things than the manager and he shouldn't let the manager butt in.

Now the field manager's job, I insist, is to have absolute control of the playing personnel and everything that happens on the field. The rule book says so. He knows better than anyone what position the team is weak in, if any, and he knows what players to trade off and where a trade would help the team most. He knows more about playing baseball—usually from several years' experience at it—than anybody else.

So why can't the field manager manage the team and the business manager handle the business end? I'll guarantee you that if John McGraw was living today—and able to manage—there wouldn't be many general managers around.

But general managers just have to second-guess. Afterwards, that is, when they've had a half hour to study the situation. Now if a manager had a pencil and piece of paper like those fellows in the press box, then the managers wouldn't make many mistakes, either. But they have to make split-second decisions all day long. This isn't a game of checkers, like general managers try to make it seem; you don't have all day to study. They're just like the people who drive to the scene of a car accident and study the tire tracks and see how the wreck could have been avoided. Hell, just about anything can be avoided later.

I'm not some old sourpuss who wouldn't go along with anything the general manager suggests. In fact, I think it's O.K. for a general manager to put on special nights to attract people in the minor leagues. One night in 1938 when I was managing the Chattanooga Lookouts in the Southern Association I took part in a little show that I never would have in the majors.

Joe Engel, the president of the Chattanooga team and a great promoter, asked me if I'd mind a "Rogers Hornsby Night" in a game against Memphis. I said O.K. and agreed to play 5 innings. I went to the plate to take the line-up to the umpire, then I looked around. There had been a lot of publicity in the papers about me arguing with Judge Landis, the baseball commissioner, about playing horses. Engel had a little jockey with a long cap, who weighed about 75 pounds, ride out an old sway-back

The General Problem—General Managers

plow horse so skinny he could hardly walk—let alone run. The horse was one of my presents. They had a little ceremony and the pictures went on the Associated Press newspaper wire all over the country, and I understand Judge Landis got all excited.

Engel pulled some great promotions to get people interested in minor-league baseball. He'd have elephant races around the ball park; have homing pigeons taking off during a game and returning at a game the next night. One night he even had some old hermit out of the Tennessee hills bury himself at the ball park in a coffin he had made himself. That's fine for the minor leagues. But not in the major leagues, where Bill Veeck, Jr., does too much silly stuff With our national pastime. Veeck, in my opinion, is a perfect example of a front-office man who interferes too much with the manager.

Even though I thought Engel helped baseball, there was one time in the minor leagues when I sure didn't go along with the script. After the Texas League suspended play in 1943 because of World War II, I went down to the Mexican League to manage the Vera Cruz team which played out of Mexico City. Jorge Pasquel owned the Vera Cruz team and 4 other teams in the league. We'd play on Thursday, Saturday and Sunday. Jorge always wanted the home team to win on Thursday, the visiting team to win on Saturday. He didn't give a damn who won on Sunday since the series would be all even and everybody who could get hold of some pesos would go to the game and make him some money.

We were playing Puebla in the second game of a series and my team had already won the first game. But we were behind by 3 runs, 16-13, going into the last of the ninth in the Saturday game. We got the bases loaded,

101

then some little Mexican who spoke both Spanish and English came up to me at third base where I was coaching. He said that Jorge Pasquel wanted me to pinch-hit.

I hadn't batted in a professional game for nearly 2 years, but I knew I could hit that little left-hander who was pitching for Puebla. He looked like a little banty rooster and didn't throw hard. So he ran the count to 2 and 0 and threw down in with a "fast" one. I laid into the pitch and hit it over the right-center-field fence. That made my team the winner 17-16.

Those little Mexicans went wild. They chased me around the bases and some of them tried to stuff those pesos in my pockets. They threw fruit at the other team. When I touched home plate they carried me off on their shoulders like one of those bullfighters, and right over to the front of Pasquel's box. Pasquel looked like Pancho Villa with an army surrounding him. He was about as excited, too.

"That was a good heet, Mr. Hornsby," Jorge told me sarcastically, "but we win! We win series too quick!"

"If you didn't want to win," I yelled, "you sure as hell picked the wrong pinch hitter."

That should have taught even the Mexican League front office not to butt in.

Getting back to the major leagues. Another front-office man who is too publicity minded, although he gets his publicity by talking instead of using silly carnival stuff like Veeck, is Frank Lane. I didn't work for him when he was general manager of the Cardinals, White Sox, Indians or Athletics. But I didn't have to. It's obvious the way he operates.

The General Problem—General Managers

Now here's what Lane says about managers: "A manager is the world's worst judge of talent. He remembers one play—either one great play or one lousy play a guy made. The general manager takes a more sensible approach and considers all the other games a guy plays. The big question with managers is what the hell do they have to manage? Well then, does the general manager have the most to do with winning? Very much so."

My, my, now, isn't that a brilliant statement. They played professional baseball 100 years in the National League before they ever heard of general managers. And now Lane makes it clear he thinks general managers should come along and manage from the press box.

Anyone could have received a good education on Lane the night the Cleveland Indians played the Chicago White Sox late in the 1959 season. Lane, who was general manager of the Indians then, sat down in the far end of the Cleveland press box. "I have to keep away from down there," he was saying (and his remarks were recorded).

"When I get excited the writers take down everything I say and then it's a big story. I keep away from writers."

Ye Gods!

A few minutes after the game started, Minnie Minoso of the Indians was thrown out at the plate by right fielder Al Smith. "That coach at third [Jo-Jo White] doesn't even think," Lane said. "He shouldn't have sent Minnie home. It was only a short fly. That Colavito can't drive in a run except when he drives himself in on a homer."

Then Ted Kluszewski of the White Sox was at bat with a couple of runners on. "Now they should walk him," Lane said. "It's better to pitch to the next guy, Romano, than Klu. You've got to pitch him tight or he'll knock it out of the park. That's fine, they're walking him."

Cleveland came to bat. Centerfielder Jimmy Piersall fouled off a pitch. "That looked like a bad pitch," said Lane, "and it was close enough that he had to swing. That's his job. Get a hit! Dammit, we wouldn't be two runs behind if Colavito hadn't been asleep on that hit. The White Sox have been running all season. He should have known Phillips would try to score. So he takes his time picking up the ball when he could have thrown out the guy at the plate."

Two innings later Woody Held of the Indians came to bat against Early Wynn. "That Wynn," Lane said, "he outfights you, pitches like a fox, then umpires. Notice how he hollers at the umpires. No wonder he's got the biggest strike zone in baseball."

When Chuck Tanner of the Indians pinch-hit for George Strickland in the fifth, somebody mentioned that Tanner hit a home run the first time he batted in the big leagues. "That's right," Lane growled, "and he hasn't hit one since."

Cleveland got runners on first and third, and Vic Power came to bat. "This will be a double play. I'll guarantee you that," Lane said. "All Power knows how to do is hit into double plays. See, Lopez [the White Sox manager] has moved the White Sox infield around for a double play. Look at that, would you? A damn double play. We played right into Lopez's hands. The secret of managing is not to do exactly what the other manager is set up for. So what do we have Power do? A little squeeze and the runner could have scored from third and the

The General Problem—General Managers

other guy could have moved to second. No, we hit into double plays."

In the sixth inning, John Romano of the White Sox flied out to center fielder Jimmy Piersall. "Good thing Piersall caught it. Francona or Tanner wouldn't have got it."

Then Al Smith of the White Sox hit a home run off Mudcat Grant, who was the new Cleveland pitcher. "Now isn't that something?" Laue boiled. "We use a pinch hitter for Perry, who's our Number One pitcher, and Grant there gives Smith a home run."

Then Jim Rivera of the White Sox hit a home run. "There should be an automatic fine for pitching fast balls to Rivera and Smith. They couldn't hit a curve with a bass fiddle and they murder fast balls. What do we do? Give them nice fast balls."

Then Phillips got a single. "That should be enough for Grant. Now if we just hadn't taken out Perry."

Pitcher Jack Harshman was sent in to pinch-hit in the Cleveland half of the seventh inning. "This really is something," Lane said. "Harshman couldn't hit me. He's hitting—you know what—one-sixty-one. Gordon's the only one who believes Harshman can hit. Why didn't he use this Dillard? He can hit."

When Vic Power came up again, Lane said: "Now he couldn't hit a homer if the fence was behind second base."

When the game was finally over—and Chicago had clinched the pennant—somebody asked Lane if he had fired Joe Gordon as Indian manager.

"I would say so," Lane said.

The next day Lane held a press conference and announced his selection of a manager for 1960. He rehired Joe Gordon the day after he fired him!

General managers, or business managers, haven't always had the authority they have today. In the days when I was playing, the club owner was usually a rabid baseball fan who lived and died baseball and worked directly with the team. Most of today's owners are too busy in their regular businesses to become involved directly with their teams—they usually buy ball clubs for publicity or as a hobby. Compare the Pittsburgh Pirates' two championship teams, for instance. John Galbreath, who is president of the Pirates, does over $100,000,000 worth of business annually building skyscrapers like the 45-story Socony Mobil Building across from Grand Central Station in New York. He also owns two horse farms—Darley Dan—and has some of the best thoroughbreds in the country. Naturally he wants to see them run in big-stake races. He doesn't have time to look after the details of a baseball front office.

Now Barney Dreyfuss, who built some great Pirate teams back in the early 1900's, is typical of the old-time owners. Dreyfuss was a German immigrant who saved his money, ran the Louisville Colonels, then later got control of the Pirates. He made baseball his life, and you couldn't take a magazine out of the office without his knowing it. And he did everything he could to improve baseball. When it was obvious that the Pirates were going to win the 1903 National League pennant, Dreyfuss got together with Henry Killilea, owner of the Boston Pilgrims of the American League, and they agreed to play

The General Problem—General Managers

in an exhibition series which they called the "World Series."

Take Phillip K. Wrigley, who owns the Chicago Cubs. His father, William Wrigley, Jr., was always around the park when I managed the Cubs in 1930-32, even though Bill Veeck, Sr., was the business manager and president. Mr. Wrigley loved baseball, too. He'd go to spring training and always beat the players getting onto the field.

But his son doesn't see 4 or 5 Cub games a year. He's got the Wrigley Company, which is the world's largest chewing-gum outfit, and I guess that's enough to worry about. So he needs somebody to look after the business end of the Cubs for him, and this is the kind of situation that has created the general manager's job.

Nevertheless that doesn't mean Wrigley doesn't like to manage the team. He has 9 or 10 coaches who shift back and forth from the minor leagues, taking turns running the Cubs. They all sit around and compare ideas. You can't run a club like that. A baseball club has to be run like an umpire runs a game—the manager has to be the absolute boss. And if there's interference throw the bum out. There's nothing wrong with having 10 coaches to teach young players if there is a job for each of them. But make one man the manager or head coach.

Charles Finley of the Kansas City Athletics is another example of an owner who likes to manage the team. In fact he said during the 1961 season that Hank Bauer was a good manager. "He's very cooperative." And Bauer said Finley liked to make a lot of playing decisions and even help pick the line-up. It looked like the owner was managing the team, too. The A's were so far down in the

My War with Baseball

cellar that about the only time the players had an even break was in an intrasquad game.

Actually Finley is like many of today's owners. He made his money in another business—insurance—and admitted when he bought the Kansas City franchise that he knew very little about running a ball club. So that's why he wanted Frank Lane to be his general manager. Now Lane, who likes to talk better than any old woman, must have been the country's most frustrated guy during the 1961 season. Finley would hardly let him announce the weather. The things they pulled when they parted company were the worst bush-league displays I've seen. I love the game and hate to see this kind of thing happen. When Finley hired Lane he announced, "I'm getting the best man in baseball." Four months later he was calling Lane the lousiest.

When I was managing I always tried to find players who I thought could help us, then tell the general manager, who would take care of all the technicalities of getting them. Actually a general manager or anyone who sits up in that box can't always tell just by looking at a player what he's capable of doing or not doing. Same as a scout can't measure a kid's determination.

I understand that George Weiss never butted into Casey Stengel's business when they worked together on the New York Yankees. The Yankees had the personnel to do about anything, and Casey played the way most managers want to do to win—the percentage way.

Branch Rickey is another front-office man who has made a tremendous contribution to baseball. He's the kind of man who should be a general manager. He was a ballplayer and a manager. He knew baseball. Nobody ever heard of a big farm system until Rickey started it with the Cardinals. And you'd have to say his farm system was mainly responsible for the Dodgers' and Pirates' World Series championships in recent years. He found out what players were needed and got them. He didn't tell the manager how to manage. Which is the way it should be. Rickey also started "Ladies' Day" and the "Knothole Day."

I ran into front-office bossing the second year I was manager—in 1926 with the Cardinals. It was near the end of the season and I told Sam Breadon, the owner, that it looked like we could win the pennant and that he should cancel three exhibition games we had scheduled. It was a tight race, too. We led the Reds by only a game. Breadon said he would do what he could to get out of the exhibitions, which was the right thing to do if he wanted to win the pennant instead of having a nice exhibition schedule.

We played morning and afternoon games in Pittsburgh and lost the morning game 1 to 0 when Allen Sothoron, one of my top pitchers, made a throwing error to first base. We were having sandwiches and milk between games when Breadon came into the clubhouse and said belligerently, "You're going to play those exhibitions, Hornsby, and that's final." All the players heard him.

"Hell, that's all right with me," I said back. "We get a total of three thousand dollars for three games and take the chance of getting some players hurt on those minor-league fields. But if you want to take a chance of kicking away a half million dollars for winning the pennant for those silly exhibition games, then I'm not going to play all my regulars."

My War with Baseball

We played those 3 exhibitions, against Syracuse, our farm team, Hartford and New Haven. Sure enough, one of my top players, left fielder Chick Hafey, got all banged up and had to miss the next 3 game series with Boston.

Nearly cost us the pennant.

6. Don't Kill the Umpire

THERE are two things that are safe to predict in baseball: (1) They have a World Series after the regular season ends; and (2) some griper will claim that umpires are killing baseball. Nobody, it seems, likes umpires. They never have. They never will. Umpires are just like policemen. A cop could jump in the river to save a child from drowning and the mother would be liable to ask, "Where's his cap?" Umpires are unquestionably as important as players and more important than a lot of them. Now wouldn't baseball be a fine game without umpires?

I've never met an umpire who wasn't fair about listening to a legitimate complaint. That old line that goes "Talking to an umpire is like talking to a brick wall" is silly, as far as I'm concerned. In all my big-league career I was thrown out of only one game for arguing with an ump—and he admitted he was wrong and let me back in the game.

I was playing for the Cardinals when I was involved in two very close plays at first base. I contended I was safe both times, and griped a little bit each time to Cy Pfirman, a rookie umpire who was making the calls at first. The third time I Was absolutely convinced that I was safe—and I argued. Since I had been complaining on the

Don't Kill the Umpire

two previous plays, Cy threw me out of the game for squawking on the third time.

But the late Bill Klem, the umpire-in-chief who was working behind home plate, came out and said, "Cy, this fellow Hornsby doesn't kick unless he has a kick coming. You'll learn that later on." Then Klem told Pfirman to put me back in the game.

Umpires don't like to throw players and managers out of games. They're not like some gun-crazy cowboy who kept notches on his pistol for the number of people he shot. They don't keep records or win any prizes for throwing out players. A manager, coach or player always puts himself out of a game.

Jocko Conlan, a National League umpire, will tell you that. "I'll always listen to a fair argument," Jocko says. "But when a player or manager argues just to be arguing, or tries to show me up in front of forty thousand people, or calls me all the dirty names he knows, I don't stand for that. I demand respect from players and managers."

Now don't get me wrong. You don't have to bow down to umpires like privates to three-star generals. If there was an umpire working behind the plate who I was positive gave the pitchers the best of the decisions on high pitches, then I'd try to use the best high-ball pitcher I had available. I think players have a perfect right to complain to umpires if they are convinced the ump is making mistakes. Sometimes it helps to complain. Occasionally it makes an umpire wonder "Maybe I did make a mistake." And he'll be more alert the next time the same situation comes up. A constant and loudmouthed griper, though, isn't going to get any consideration from any umpire. The only opinions that umpires respect and listen to are from those who kick only when they have a kick coming.

I'm not defending the guys who couldn't tell a strike if they saw one in slow motion, then jump up and down like maniacs to cover up for their own shortcomings. Or run around like chickens with their heads cut off trying to alibi. Al Forman, a fairly new umpire in the National League, sums up the situation pretty well. "The smart hitters don't bother umpires," Al says. "They know we aren't infallible and they know they aren't, either. It's the weight hitters—the guys averaging their own weights—not the .300 hitters who give you a hard time."

And there are some constant kickers, too. Here's the alibi that's sort of standard for base runners getting thrown out on a close play while trying to take an extra base, and sometimes killing a good rally. "That damn ump wasn't anywhere near the play. We have to be in shape to play ball. Why can't umps be in shape? Why?"

When I managed, I always told my players that I definitely didn't believe in complaining to umpires just to be complaining. And I told them not to, either. "I'll think a lot more of you as a ballplayer," I always said, "if you admit your mistakes rather than try to alibi by blaming it on the umpires. It takes a man to admit he did something wrong. Any coward can alibi."

I've continually seen players called out on a third strike, coming back to the dugout whining about the umpire missing calls all day. "Umpire missed it, hell," I'd tell them. "If the ball is close enough to be called a strike, it's close enough to swing. That's the way I batted. Did all right, too."

Cal Hubbard, a good umpire, had the same theory. "I'm an umpire capable of making mistakes," he would tell gripers, "so if it's close, you'd better swing at it."

The one thing I used to hammer in my players' heads was that too much griping at the umpires really hurts the player in the long run. Then when you do have a legitimate kick the umpires won't pay any attention to you. Bill Veeck might not be too far wrong on what he charges in one of his annual blasts at umpires. Veeck says, "Umpires unconsciously give the hitters with a reputation for a good eye—such as Ted Williams and Eddie Yost—breaks on close balls and strikes. Umpires figure Williams or Yost would have swung at the pitch had it been a strike. That's one reason Yost annually leads the league in bases on balls."

It's only human nature that nobody—even an umpire—is going out of his way to be nice to any player who calls him a "blind son of a gun," or asks "Where's your Seeing Eye dog, Ump?" Or sneers, "Drunk again, huh?" Neither Williams nor Yost—nor the other good hitters—ever go after umpires with smart-aleck stuff like that. I know that if I was umpiring I wouldn't lean over backward for any kind of habitual griper.

Personally I never made much noise over balls and strikes. I used to tell umpires that it was O.K. with me to miss the first two strikes, but they'd better make damn sure on the third one. I batted that way, too. Then if they did call what I considered a questionable strike—even if it seemed real bad—I didn't go wild. It doesn't do any good, anytime, to yell like an idiot or try to impress the people in the stands. I'd simply say, "Where was that pitch?"

My War with Baseball

Every umpire always told me about a pitch in a gentlemanly manner. They would say, "Inside, couple of inches above your knee." Or "Just caught the outside corner right on the top of your letters." Umpires were in a much better position to see the pitch than I was. And I feel confident that this attitude toward umpires helped me—I got all the good advice I could. I'm sure I couldn't have improved my hitting by popping off about the umpire being one of the original three blind mice. Or telling him to buy a license tag for his so-called Seeing Eye dog, like some guys do. I wouldn't hesitate to recommend my approach to umpires to any young hitter today. I feel confident that I had a decent reputation with them.

Take the time I was playing for the New York Giants in 1927. We were playing the Brooklyn Dodgers. Jim Elliott, a left-hander, was pitching for the Dodgers, and Hank DeBerry was catching. Cy Pfirman was working behind the plate. Elliott seemed to be having a little trouble with his control, so naturally I wasn't going after everything he pitched. Elliott and DeBerry griped on every pitch. Real hard, too. Finally the count went to 3 and 2. Elliott laid one down the middle and I was lucky enough to knock the ball into the right-field stands for a home run. Then Pfirman trotted about halfway to the pitcher's mound and hollered at Elliott: "Mr. Hornsby will let you know when the ball is over the plate."

That's the way umpires are. They don't give a player the worst of a decision on purpose. They have the toughest decisions in the world to make. With only a split second to do this they can of course make mistakes just as easily as a guy wheeling on a double play. Every umpire will average over 10,000 decisions, either behind the plate or on the bases, every season. Every decision is questionable—to the thousands of fans in the stands, to the two teams, to the sports writers or to the front-office people.

Everybody at the park is against the umpire. If an umpire gets hit hard by a line drive or a foul tip, the crowd doesn't shut up like it does when a player gets hurt, then applaud for him when he gets up. They laugh! Like the umpire was a goddam clown. The highest compliment an umpire can get from anybody in the stands is absolutely NOTHING—no boos or insults from the crowd, no bitching or nasty insults from the players, no bottles thrown at him, nobody threatening him.

Even if an umpire makes the biggest mistake in the world I don't believe in ten guys charging onto the field waving their arms and trying to humiliate him. Most players wouldn't take abuse like that if they were umpiring. What do you think a player would do today if he made an obvious error, and, say, the plate umpire—or even the player's own manager—stormed out to the middle of the field screaming and ridiculing him in front of the entire crowd? He'd go nuts. Couldn't take it.

Umpires go through that kind of harassment every day and I think they deserve more respect than they're shown. I always discussed the plays with umpires in the right tone of voice—no screaming or gesturing. You can expect errors from umpires—the same as players. The decisions may be wrong, but in their own hearts they don't think they have made a mistake. And they make fewer mistakes in their jobs than players do. Bill Klem, the most famous of all umpires, said right before he died, in 1951, "I never really thought I missed a play in my life." And Klem umpired for 36 years in the National League and worked in 18 World Series.

Taking charge of the game, I think, is the No. 1 rule for being a good umpire. Ex-umpire Emmett (Red) Ormsby says, "I umpired in the American League for nineteen years and I know you definitely can't do a top-notch job unless you feel you are the most important person on the field. If umpires didn't have the absolute backing of the league, players would run over them. If an umpire yields an inch he's in trouble. Players are always trying to control the game.

"When Ban Johnson was the American League president he would write sharp letters to us umpires if we went over ten days without throwing a player out of a game. 'Kick somebody out of a game tomorrow,' Ban would say, 'so they know who's boss. If they gripe I'll straighten them out.'"

Of course some people don't like anybody who is boss or has authority, and that's what makes umpiring even harder today. When I was a kid and there was trouble between the schoolteacher and a kid, the parents backed up the teacher. They back up the kid today—and usually try to cause the teacher trouble. So what can you expect?

Every year a weekly baseball paper conducts a poll to pick out the "most sarcastic umpire," "funniest umpire," "most belligerent umpire," "toughest umpire" and junk like that. I've never met a tough, belligerent umpire in the major leagues. They're all gentlemen. They're human beings. They dress the same way as other people; eat the same kind of foods; even live in houses like other people; send their kids to school, too.

If anybody wants to pick a "most belligerent" or "toughest umpire" every year I'll guarantee anybody I can get along with them. The umpire they single out for

Don't Kill the Umpire

being the most uncooperative or toughest doesn't enjoy being that way. He wants to umpire—not fight.

Even most of the umpires violently disapprove of these polls. Take the case of Al Barlick, who was voted the best umpire in the National League for 1961. Al won the top rating in six categories—best caller of balls and strikes; best on making calls on the bases; best knowledge of rules; best at being in the right position; most highly respected; most serious minded; and he finished in a tie for most deliberate on making decisions. Of course they picked some other umpires; "most diplomatic," "most easygoing," "biggest grandstander," "most sarcastic," "quickest," "worst pop-off," "neatest," "most difficult to talk to," "most even tempered," and "least likely to eject players and managers." Well, if this poll was something nice you'd think the guy voted No. 1 would stand up and cheer. That umpire is Al Barlick. Al doesn't approve of such polls and I don't either.

"I say the very idea of the ratings is unfair," Barlick says, "and not only unfair but a disgrace to baseball. What's so unfair is that the ratings branded some hard-working umpires who are always trying to do a good job. Tell me what in the world does neatness have to do with sound umpiring on the field?

"Why take one umpire—and a good umpire, too—and single him out as the biggest so-and-so? Or biggest grand-stander? What do they mean by respect? Taking all that filthy stuff from somebody trying to get something for nothing or alibi.

"Just because certain umpires refuse to take that stuff does not make them 'sarcastic' or 'belligerent' or 'biggest grandstander.' It sure doesn't. I like to be respected—but

My War with Baseball

not at the expense of my fellow umpires and their self-respect. Besides, most of the people who vote in this so-called exclusive poll are sports writers. They're not on the field—real close up on every play the umpire makes. How do they know Whether the umpire missed one or not? They don't—not by a long shot. How do they know who is the 'most belligerent'? They don't."

The only time anyone meets a belligerent or tough umpire—and I know this from plenty of experience—is when some player tries to humiliate him and calls him a "blind son of a bitch," and dirt like that. No human being is going to take that kind of treatment. Especially anyone with guts, and it takes a helluva lot of guts to umpire. Sort of like somebody volunteering to be a human dart board at a charity event. A person has to have a special disposition to become an umpire. I know I couldn't be one. Not that I couldn't make decisions. But I just wouldn't stand there when some two-bit .190 hitter used all the cuss words he's ever heard in the restrooms in calling me a blind ol' goat. I'd probably grab a bat and start swinging at him myself. I never took that kind of abuse from anyone and I don't think umpires should have to. One time, though, an umpire didn't take it.

Billy Jurges, who was playing for the New York Giants, was involved in a loud, arm-waving argument with the home-plate and third-base umpires in questioning a home run hit by Harry Craft of the Cincinnati Reds in 1939. When Umpire George Magerkurth moved over from first base to get in the discussion Jurges got smart and told Magerkurth to mind his own business over at first base.

"This is my business, you little squirt," Magerkurth told Jurges.

"Don't spit in my face," Jurges yelled, among a lot of other things.

"Get your face out of here and I won't be spitting in it," Magerkurth hollered.

"How'd you like for me to spit in your face?" Jurges egged on.

"I'd just like to see you try it," Magerkurth said.

Jurges tried, all right. Hit him right above the eye. Magerkurth punched him right in the stomach—which led to a good fist fight, and cost Magerkurth a $250 fine and a 10-day suspension administered by Ford Frick, who then was president of the National League.

Probably the biggest fight between a player and umpire took place between Umpire Billy Evans and Ty Cobb. One day Cobb didn't like one of Evans' calls. And Evans didn't like what Cobb called him. They agreed to meet under the stands after the game.

Cobb loved to fight. Evans didn't exactly hate to mix it up—he'd been a boxer while attending Cornell. So Evans asked Cobb how he liked to fight.

"I fight to kill," Ty said.

The fight, I'm told, lasted for 45 minutes. Evans landed some good left jabs, which he must have learned while boxing. But he soon wore down, and Cobb got on top of him and pounded away. When the fight got too bloody the players pulled them apart.

Back in 1909—six years before I entered the major leagues—Kid Elberfeld of the New York Yankees must have really said something hard to Umpire Carroll (Tim) Hurst. Hurst punched Elberfeld in the face—then threw him out of the game. But Hurst got thrown out permanently a few weeks later for spitting at Eddie Collins of the Philadelphia Athletics. Collins really liked to bait Hurst. And Hurst had the habit, they say, of calling a runner out at first base on obvious plays before the first baseman caught the ball. One day Collins and Harry Davis, the A's first baseman, worked up a little gag where Collins faked a throw and Davis pretended to catch the throw. Hurst is supposed to have signaled "out," then corrected himself when Collins held up the ball, laughing. Collins took the ball and tried to show Hurst up before the crowd.

Umps had to be pretty tough back then. People were damn tough on them. One publication even ran a regular feature called, "How to Needle the Umpire." The papers called umpires everything, and this clipping, taken from *Leslie's Weekly* of May 20, 1909, is sort of typical:

> Messrs. Truby and Rigler were the official representatives of the National League on the field. Of Mr. Rigler, it is known that he came to the National League with a reputation of having the physical qualifications of a prize fighter. Nothing was said of his mental ability at the time, though much has been said on the subject since he joined us. Mr. Truby is entirely new to us, and he gets to be more and more of a joy from day to day. It has been the destiny of the writer to be hooked up in the games where these two gentlemen have officiated ever since the season opened, and they form one of the most interesting teams we have seen since Punch and Judy quit.

Sportswriters have asked me many times who I considered the funniest umpire of all time. I always said, "None of them." No major-league umpire wants to be known as funny. They're on the field on business, and they're dead serious. If they wanted to clown they'd try show business. Oh, I'm not saying umpires don't have a sense of humor. They have to have some kind of special humor—or whatever you want to call it—to take all the abuse they do. Some umpires' motions on balls and strikes or calling a man out might appear funny to some people.

Down in the Southern Association in 1949 an umpire did put on a little act. Harry Sam Johnson, an umpire who got the nickname of "Steamboat" because of his foghorn voice, was led out on the field at New Orleans by a Seeing Eye dog. The police had handcuffs on Harry and he wore dark glasses. The other umpires joined the act by booing the fans. Of course that was a team promotion to sort of pay tribute to Steamboat. He'd been umpiring 30 years in the league.

Bill Byron also gained some sort of notoriety for being a singing umpire back in the 1920's. Any time a manager gave him too much trouble and he decided to throw him out, he is supposed to have sung:

> To the clubhouse you must go
> You must go
> You must go
> To the clubhouse you must go,
> My fair MANAGER!

Or if batters raised too much hell over a called third strike and were really difficult, he'd sing this little verse:

> Let me tell you something, son,
> Before you get much older.
> You can't hit the ball
> With that big bat on your shoulder.

My War with Baseball

I guess that was supposed to be funny, but I never heard him sing it to me or my players.

There's that old gag they tell just about every time they introduce an umpire to make a speech during the off season. We'll call the umpire Walter Lively. The toastmaster gets up and introduces Mr. Lively as the guest speaker. "Now," says the toastmaster, laughing, "Mr. Lively here was umpiring against the Dodgers, see. And the centerfielder of the Dodgers was giving him all kinds of trouble and the like. So Mr. Lively here throws this cussin' Dodger centerfielder out, see.

"Now this really starts a fuss. So the manager of the Dodgers—you know all about him—charges Mr. Lively here and demands to know why Mr. Lively threw out his star centerfielder.

" 'Oh, you've got me all wrong,' Mr. Lively here says, 'I didn't throw him out of the game.'

" 'The hell you didn't,' the Dodger manager screams back.

" 'No, you're wrong,' Mr. Lively here says back to the Dodger manager, 'I excused him because he was sick.'

" 'What the hell do you mean sick?' the manager screamed. 'He didn't say anything to me about being sick. Never mentioned it to the doc.'

" 'Well, he came up to me of his own free will,' " the toastmaster says, patting his sides and reaching for another drink. Then the toastmaster points over to the umpire—Mr. Lively. People are supposed to laugh—and lots of them do—but I figure if a guy does anything he should throw something at the toastmaster.

Don't Kill the Umpire

I didn't pay any attention to the so-called funny umpire stores when I was playing or managing. I didn't pay any more attention to the umpire baiters than I did to the corny comedians. Baseball was my profession, and I didn't let anything interfere with my job—except when I got fired. People could call me anything they wanted. I didn't hear most of them. Didn't have time.

My theory was that a person can only concentrate on one thing at a time. If you use up all of your energy during a ball game trying to think up something funny or nasty to holler at an umpire, you're only hurting yourself in the long run. There's only one way to hit: keep studying the pitcher. They change during a game. There's only one way to be a manager—keep studying both pitchers. When I was a coach for the Chicago Cubs in 1958 one of the Cubs' leading players came back to the bench after striking out against the Milwaukee Braves and asked, "Who's that out there pitching, anyway?" That's common today. It's a darn good thing I wasn't managing.

When Bobby Bragan was managing the 1957 Pittsburgh Pirates he really liked to bait umpires. Liked to pick on Frank Dascoli. One day in the Polo Grounds the New York Giants were blasting the Pirate pitcher and there wasn't much question about taking him out. So Bragan strolled out to the mound and called everybody in for a conference.

"Think I ought to leave him in?" Bragan asked Dale Long, the first baseman.

"I would," Long answered.

"What about you, Dick?" Bragan asked shortstop Dick Groat.

"I wouldn't take him out."

"Maz," Bragan asked second baseman Bill Mazeroski, "What do you think?"

"I'd go with him a little longer."

By now Dascoli, the plate umpire, was out on the mound yelling, "Let's play ball." Which is what he should have been doing.

Bragan, though, gave him a funny grin.

"You're catching, Shep," Bragan said to catcher Jack Shepard. "Does he still have it?"

"He's O.K.," Shephard said, "I'd stick with him a little longer."

"Let's go," the umpire said.

"What about you, Frank?" Bragan asked third baseman Frank Thomas.

"Let him stay in," Frank said.

"Now are you ready to go?" Dascoli said.

"Now what about it, Ump?" Bragan snarled. "Think he's got his stuff, or should we take him out?"

"That's your job, not mine," Dascoli answered. "But do something."

It wasn't Bragan's job very much longer, though.

A few days later Bragan was propped up on the steps of the dugout of County Stadium in Milwaukee when he told the clubhouse boy, "Get me a hot dog and a Coke."

Two outs later Bragan was out in the middle of the field protesting a foul-ball call. When he finished his gripe Bragan strolled back to the dugout. "All they had was orange juice," the clubhouse boy said. "I'll take it back if you don't want it, Mr. Bragan."

"That's fine, son," Bragan grinned, "real fine." Then Bragan proceeded sort of nonchalantly to the pitcher's mound and offered all the umpires—Frank Secory, Stan Landis, and Dascoli—a sip of his orange juice.

A few days later Bragan got fired. Oh, now it wasn't his fault. He swears it wasn't. "Dascoli was too quick to get mad. Especially in my case. He's too willing to throw a guy out of a game."

In my opinion this kind of incident is a disgrace to baseball. All it does is get a manager thrown out of a game, and he does a helluva lot of good taking a shower while the team is playing.

John McGraw had the reputation of being the all-time umpire baiter, but I maintain that's a myth. There are stories circulating that McGraw would pretend he fainted because an umpire's decision supposedly was so shocking. I never saw him do anything like this when I played for him in 1927—or any other time. He was much too serious a manager to pull such tricks. Umpires knew they wouldn't have any trouble from McGraw until they missed a big play. Then they could expect him to raise holy hell. Connie Mack had the same idea about umpires. He got thrown out of a game in his first year as manager, but never got thrown out again. And he managed the Philadelphia Athletics for 50 years.

A fellow really has to be dedicated to, and in love with, baseball to become a big-league umpire. There are some players in the major leagues with a half-hearted attitude, but there certainly aren't any among the umpires.

My War with Baseball

Nowadays some players get right into the big leagues in a couple of seasons and draw big salaries—like bonuses—while they're getting there. But an umpire has a long, rough road of at least 6 or 7 years in the minors at low salaries before he gets to the major leagues—if he gets there at all.

Take the case of Terry Tata, a young fellow who started out recently in the Class D Midwest League. He's in his early twenties and knows he won't be able to get to the major leagues—even if he's good enough—before he's thirty years old. Probably later. Terry draws $300 a month, which is a little less than $75 a week. He works with only one other umpire, and many times during the summer he and his fellow umpire will work a night game in, say, Kokomo, Indiana, grab a quick sandwich and bottle of milk, then drive to Dubuque, Iowa, which is 400 miles away. And the road isn't any prize, either. Then they umpire a game that night. He's a smart kid, and I'm sure he could make much more money than he takes home from umpiring. All umpires go through this same apprenticeship. They have to prove that they are the best in the world at their profession.

"Umpiring is just something we love to do," says Ed Hurley, an umpire some people have been after lately. "Few ballplayers are in the game just for money. They don't play for nothing, I know, but most of them enjoy playing. Love it. I love to umpire. I know I'm not going to make any friends—all I can do is make enemies. Then it gets you after a while. I can't go home and relax. I take the game to bed with me. To be a good umpire, it's got to be like a religion with you."

I consider Jocko Conlan one of the best umpires in the game today, and funny thing about it, I helped him get

Don't Kill the Umpire

his first umpiring "assignment." I was the manager of the St. Louis Browns, and we were playing the Chicago White Sox when Umpire Red Ormsby fainted because of the heat. We needed an umpire.

Conlan was an outfielder with the White Sox and volunteered. People thought I was crazy for allowing a White Sox outfielder to umpire, but I agreed anyway. Jocko did a good job in that game and has done a good job ever since. He's a take-charge-of-the-game umpire, and that's the kind you need.

Nevertheless, everybody, everywhere, is always after umpires.

People are even trying to replace umpires with machines. A Long Island engineer has patented a machine, which includes some television equipment, that supposedly calls balls and strikes. And Bill Veeck, the umpire hater, installed an "Eye-in-the-Sky" camera in Comiskey Park when he was president of the Chicago White Sox. "I know electronic devices aren't difficult to set up," Veeck maintains. "There's no reason why baseball—like horse racing—can't have cameras to produce photos of every close play on the spot. The Eye-in-the-Sky, with its thousand frames each second, catches every nuance of a situation. And it keeps umpires on their toes. Once they found out I was photographing their calls they obviously hustled more."

But if baseball used cameras instead of umpires a helluva lot of people would be up that well-known creek without a paddle—they wouldn't have any umpires to complain about.

There are four baseball players living who have hit .400—and here we are: Bill Terry, Ted Williams, myself, and George Sisler.

That's me (back row, fifth from right), when we trained in Orange, Texas, in 1921. I won the batting championship that season for the second time in my career.

In 1926, when I managed the St. Louis Cardinals to their first world championship.

John McGraw, the famous manager of the New York Giants, and I get together when I was player-manager of the 1926 St. Louis Cardinals. And if anybody thought I was a tough manager, they should have played for McGraw. I did—the next year when I was suddenly traded by the Cardinals.

UNITED PRESS PHOTOS

After spending all of my career with the Cardinals, I suddenly found myself swinging a bat for the Giants in 1927, and people wanted to know how different things were. Wasn't any different to me. I just played ball and tended to my own business.

William Wrigley, Jr. (left), William Veeck, Sr. (right) and myself are all smiles when I was picked to manage the Cubs. But Veeck, who was the president and general manager, wanted to manage too and naturally we didn't get along.

UNITED PRESS PHOTOS

I take my swing during the 1929 season with the Cubs. Had a pretty good year—was voted the league's most valuable player and we won the pennant.

UNITED PRESS PHOTO

As you can see, there's no big conversation between Charley Grimm (left), first baseman and manager of the Cubs, and myself, playing for the Cardinals the year after I was Cub manager, in this 1933 game. Of course, I never spoke to opposing players anyway unless they spoke first.

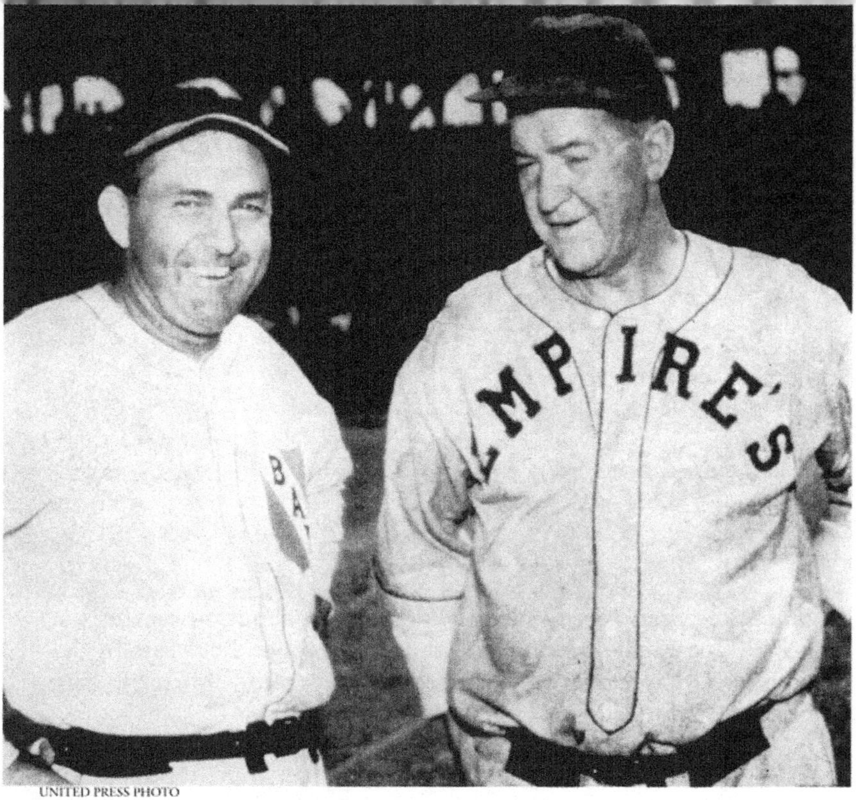

UNITED PRESS PHOTO

Grover Cleveland Alexander (right), whom I regard as the greatest pitcher of all time, plays against me again. This time it's in a semi-pro tournament in Denver when we both are near the end of our playing days.

AP WIREPHOTO

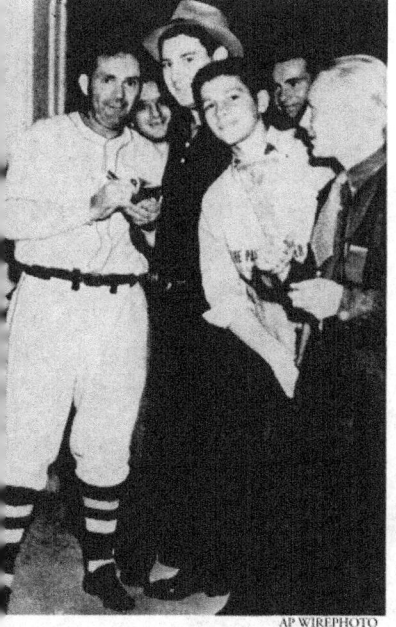

I always told players I managed that they didn't owe me the first obligation to hustle. They owed it to the fans. And I always tried to sign as many autographs as I had time.

Since there were several rumors in the papers about me playing the horses, Joe Engle, president of the Chattanooga Lookouts in the Southern Association, presented me a plow horse during ceremonies for "Rogers Hornsby Night" in 1938.

They claimed I was a "slave driver" in spring training when I managed the 1952 St. Louis Browns. We always had a meeting before practice and we just practiced. We weren't at any sun resort.

Photographer Ernest Sisto caught me in a baseball moment of truth when I was swinging for St. Louis in 1952.

UNITED PRESS PHOTOS

As long as players hustled and gave baseball everything, they never had any trouble with me as a manager. From the looks of this shot taken when I managed the Reds in 1953, I wasn't too unhappy.

7. Salaries and Bonuses

MOST of the funny baseball stories are fiction. They usually start with an argument between a player and umpire, and by the time they get into print the stories have been exaggerated to the point where the player tosses his bat straight up. Then the umpire yells, "When that bat hits the ground you're out of the game." So the player makes a diving catch.

That story, like many in baseball, stretches the point. But it still isn't the biggest exaggeration that's printed every spring. That's the one concerning salaries. This really takes imagination—the publicity men who hit at the salary figures they want the newspapermen to guess at and print. Gullible sportswriters raced each other to the office to print stories like "Ted Williams Signs for $125,000," "Mays Gets $85,000—Tops in National League," "Musial Gets $100,000 Again!"

For the people who read this stuff and want to determine the actual salaries they should divide by three and deduct a third.

This has been one of my pet arguments for years. Baseball's front-office figures think that any time a fan reads about a player getting a lot of money it automatically sells tickets. One time an alert publicity man had a player flying back and forth arguing over $1,000 in his

Major-league clubs lure rookies with big bonuses that kill incentive.

Salaries and Bonuses

salary when the plane fare amounted to almost $500. The player lived in Venezuela.

After the season starts they announce all these fancy bonus-baby figures. I may be old-fashioned, but I don't believe headlines with a bunch of dollar signs in them create much excitement among the fans. I realize that the clubs get all kinds of publicity for the big salary talk. But I contend a player can be drawing a million dollars—with the club paying him off in silver dollars at home plate—and he won't draw his relatives to the ball park unless he does something with that bat or ball that makes him interesting to watch. Oh, a few people might come out to see a new player once, but they would be so few you probably could sit all of them on top of the bat rack. Only proven, hustling ballplayers are drawing cards.

Mentioning money, I know, isn't new in the promotion business. Movie people usually double or triple the price they pay for a book they plan to convert into a movie. Yet you can't lay all the blame on the baseball front office. It never officially announces the salary—mainly because the one in the newspaper is so much larger than the player actually gets. What it does do is plant approximate figures with the sportswriters.

A typical front-office answer to a baseball writer's question is that "We never announce salaries. That's the privacy of the player."

They start off by giving the sportswriter a figure like some junk auctioneer starting a bid on a secondhand bedroom suite. Like "So-and-so is worth fifty thousand dollars. He knows what he's worth. And he's got a contract that he is perfectly happy with."

My War with Baseball

Then the sportswriter, who usually can't raise $5 without borrowing or going home, lets his imagination run away with him. When he gets at that typewriter he goes hog wild with thousands of dollars. Like it was nothing. Makes a better story, he figures. By the time a salary gets in print a guy drawing $30,000 is getting $52,500 and wishes the sportswriters, instead of the ball club, were paying him.

Pee Wee Reese's remark about his salary when he first came up to the Brooklyn Dodgers is typical of phony-salary stories.

"I asked for nine thousand dollars," says Pee Wee, "and got seven thousand. It came out twelve thousand in the papers."

One day Biggie Garagnani, who runs Stan and Biggie's restaurant in St. Louis in partnership with Stan Musial, was having dinner in a booth with Frank Scott, a New York agent for most of the big-league players who want to endorse things for money.

"Say, Scott," Biggie asked, "does Mantle get seventy-five thousand dollars like all the papers say?"

"Unh, unh," Scott answered, shaking his head.

"Didn't think he did," Biggie said. "Stan ain't gettin' a hundred thousand, either."

Back when I was playing they didn't exaggerate on salaries and they didn't go insane over high-school players by giving outlandish bonuses. I never helped any sportswriter "guess" on my salary. They said it was "private," and I kept it that way. If the club had wanted me to announce the salary I would have. But I don't think

Salaries and Bonuses

salaries should be announced. What does it mean, anyway?

Teams would be better off if they'd forget the salary publicity. At least it wouldn't look so bad when a player has to get on a stand and swear how much he's making. In 1957, for example, the House of Representatives' Anti-trust Subcommittee held a hearing on sports. (I didn't approve of these hearings and even wrote a long letter to Congressman Emanuel Celler bragging about baseball.) One of the things that it talked about, and passed a few official reports around on, was baseball salaries.

The committee revealed that in the same year that Ted Williams of the Boston Red Sox was getting $125,000, the highest salary paid in the American League was $ 58,000. And Boston is in the American League, isn't it?

Actually, the hearings proved that ballplayers' salaries, on the average, don't put them in the same spending-money class as the President. Or Elizabeth Taylor. Here are the official salary figures of all major-league teams between 1952-56, which is the last time Congress made the clubs open up their books:

NATIONAL LEAGUE

Year	Total Salaries	Average	Median
BROOKLYN (now Los Angeles Dodgers)			
1952	357,500	14,300	8,750
1953	385,000	15,400	12,000
1954	441,500	17,660	13,500
1955	415,500	16,620	13,000
1956	472,000	18,880	14,000

My War with Baseball

Year	Total Salaries	Average	Median
CHICAGO			
1952	263,000	10,520	9,000
1953	404,500	16,180	13,000
1954	362,000	14,480	13,000
1955	303,000	12,120	12,000
1956	283,625	11,340	10,000
CINCINNATI			
1952	224,000	10,180	9,500
1953	236,000	9,830	9,000
1954	237,000	9,480	8,000
1955	274,250	10,970	9,000
1956	305,500	12,220	11,500
MILWAUKEE (Formerly Boston Braves)			
1952	279,000	12,130	7,000
1953	292,200	11,690	9,500
1954	372,750	14,910	13,000
1955	433,500	17,340	12,500
1956	437,500	17,500	13,500
NEW YORK (now San Franscisco Giants)			
1952	433,000	17,320	15,000
1953	423,500	16,940	13,000
1954	358,500	14,340	13,500
1955	428,000	17,120	16,000
1956	396,500	15,860	13,500
PHILADELPHIA			
1952	304,000	12,670	10,000
1953	321,250	13,380	11,000
1954	335,000	13,960	11,000
1955	360,250	14,410	12,000
1956	409,000	16,360	12,500
PITTSBURGH			
1952	297,000	11,880	6,000
1953	207,250	8,290	7,500
1954	208,000	9,040	8,500
1955	220,500	8,820	7,000
1956	248,500	9,940	8,000

Salaries and Bonuses

Year	Total Salaries	Average	Median
ST. LOUIS			
1952	395,000	15,800	10,000
1953	391,500	15,660	11,500
1954	398,250	15,930	9,000
1955	349,000	13,960	12,000
1956	403,000	16,120	12,000

AMERICAN LEAGUE

BOSTON			
1952	378,270	15,760	11,630
1953	425,000	15,740	11,000
1954	400,250	14,820	10,000
1955	398,000	14,210	9,500
1956	421,000	15,590	12,500
CHICAGO			
1952	264,210	11,490	10,000
1953	333,500	13,900	12,000
1954	408,000	16,320	15,000
1955	430,630	17,220	15,000
1956	438,090	17,520	16,000
CLEVELAND			
1952	442,930	17,720	16,500
1953	451,000	18,790	16,750
1954	487,050	18,040	17,500
1955	567,000	22,680	20,000
1956	444,520	18,520	18,000
DETROIT			
1952	380,230	14,620	13,130
1953	335,160	13,410	13,000
1954	278,660	12,120	10,000
1955	291,730	12,160	9,300
1956	361,770	14,470	13,000

My War with Baseball

Year	Total Salaries	Average	Median
NEW YORK			
1952	421,000	16,190	14,280
1953	438,250	16,860	14,500
1954	510,000	18,890	16,500
1955	411,500	15,830	13,000
1956	492,000	17,570	16,380
KANSAS CITY (formerly Philadelphia Athletics)			
1952	269,310	11,710	10,340
1953	272,500	11,850	10,000
1954	215,730	10,270	7,500
1955	251,440	11,430	9,250
1956	253,030	12,050	10,000
BALTIMORE (formerly St. Louis Browns			
1952	262,470	10,500	9,000
1953	292,630	12,190	10,000
1954	272,400	11,350	11,000
1955	270,750	10,830	10,000
1956	302,000	11,180	10,500
WASHINGTON			
1952	274,250	11,430	11,000
1953	251,000	11,950	12,000
1954	300,500	12,020	11,000
1955	287,500	11,500	10,000
1956	212,250	9,780	8,750

Big money today, though, is a different thing with the ridiculous bonuses being paid kids who haven't even seen a professional game in person. The big money they get is for real. Major-league clubs realize, of course, that they are being soaked pretty hard to sign some of the best high-school players. "Sometimes I wonder how stupid we can get to pay these outlandish bonuses," says John McHale, general manager of the Milwaukee Braves. "But we're stuck with it." Ford Frick, the commissioner of baseball, agrees and says flatly, "It's

Salaries and Bonuses

absolutely wrong to give an untried player all that money. It has to rob a kid of all his incentive."

Even if a club has $10,000,000 to spend on bonuses, I still maintain that it hurts itself in the long run by going wild on money. It's obvious that bonuses have killed the incentive in most kids—90 percent of the bonus players have failed. It's only human nature that a person does a better job if he knows he can earn a bonus by doing a good job rather than starting on top and working his way to the bottom. A ballplayer has to be kept sort of hungry. There's never been a boy from a rich society family who ever played big-league ball.

When I was a kid I wanted to play big-league ball when I grew up. I would have signed for practically anything. All I wanted was enough money to live on. And I didn't get much more than that—$75 a month for playing on the Denison team in the Class D Texas-Oklahoma League.

In fact I didn't get that contract handed to me on any silver platter, either. I played ball any time I could. I used to go out into the streets after dark and throw the ball up under the arc lights. Or I'd have some kids pitch to me and I'd practice my bunting. When I got a little bigger my mother made me a baseball suit out of blue flannel. Even made me some sliding pads out of some material used to make bed quilts, and sold the idea to the Wilson Company, which gave her royalties on it. They are now standard equipment with all professional players.

But when I got on this kid team named the North Side Athletics we used to ride the carline out to the edge of Fort Worth, then walk the other five miles to Rosen Heights—in the suburbs—to play. It wasn't anything like the Little Leagues or Pony Leagues today. Sometimes we didn't even have a decent ball and used tape to patch up a ball to play with.

I'll never forget that first uniform, either. I owned some pigeons and chickens and traded them to another boy in the neighborhood for a big billy goat. So the day I showed up in the uniform my mother sewed for me the goat didn't recognize me and chased me with his horns lowered. I had to jump up on a fence to get away from him.

But anyway, another boy in my neighborhood and I wanted to play ball so bad that we even answered an advertisement in a Dallas newspaper to play against the Boston Bloomer Girls. I didn't figure that I could ever get into a professional league that way. When I got the chance to try out with a pro team I was tickled to death.

Other kids who eventually became big leaguers felt the same way. They just prayed that a scout would see them and give them a chance. Today, however, fathers groom their kids to be big-league "bonus" players because they know the money is there. When the scouts come around, some of the fathers even say, "The bidding starts at fifty thousand." The father acts like a kind of auctioneer. It doesn't make any difference which club the player has a chance to go with or how big an opportunity he has.

The Kansas city Athletics have a scout named Lew Krausse, and when the A's were ready to sign his son, Lew Krausse, Jr., they had to go to $125,000 to beat out the other teams. He may have been worthy every cent. He shut out the Los Angeles Angels in his first big-league game and came back with a two-hit shutout over the

Salaries and Bonuses

Boston Red Sox a few days later. If you can sign a player who is good enough to play regular, then he isn't such a bad risk. But it's against the principles of any business organization to pay a kid $100,000 and send him to a Class D or C league and hope he will have enough determination to work his way up to the top.

I'm not trying to say that all bonus players have cashed their checks, then failed right off the bat. Harvey Kuenn, Al Kaline, Dick Groat, Jackie Jensen, Sandy Koufax, Robin Roberts, Curt Simmons, Andy Carey, Harmon Killebrew, Johnny Antonelli and Mike McCormick all got bonuses and made good. But they're a very small percentage, believe me.

These players all received reported $50,000 to $120,000 bonuses: Paul Pettit, Billy Joe Davidson, Frank Leja, Ed Cereghino, Bob Miller, Gus Keriazakos, Larry Isbell, Billy Consolo, Paul Giel, J. W. Porter, Ted Kazanski, Hugh Radcliffe, Jerry Robinson, Frank Quinn, Mike Lee, Tookie Gilbert, Tom Qualters and Jim Pyburn. I can't find any of these players on big-league rosters now.

Dick Wakefield, who got $51,000 and a new car by signing with the Detroit Tigers in 1941, makes it plain that a big bonus puts extra pressure on players. "Anytime you're a bonus player and make a mistake," Wakefield admits, "everybody gets on you. A bonus is fine—if you make good right away and never make an error. Mess up once like all the other players and the pressure is double. Few people can take that."

You'd have to say that the biggest bonus failures of all time are Davidson and Pettit—both pitchers.

My War with Baseball

The Cleveland Indians made front-page headlines all over the country in 1951 by announcing they paid a $120,000 bonus to get Davidson, a nice boy with a good fast ball. Billy Joe wasn't exactly a sensation, but he was showing some improvement in the minors when he hurt his shoulder one day and couldn't throw as hard as he once did. "I realized that I wasn't going to make the majors," Billy said, "and I had had enough of the minors." And he quit.

Pettit didn't give up as quickly, but it didn't make much difference as far as the Pirates were concerned. The last time I heard of him he was trying to become a first baseman with a Class C team. Actually he is a perfect example of how somebody can promote a bonus for a good player.

Fourteen of the 16 major-league teams made bids for Pettit, and the Pirates "won." But they had to buy the contract from Frederick Stephani, an independent Hollywood movie producer who figured Pettit was a cinch for an all-American boy role in a baseball movie. Stephani never made the movie, but he made $10,000 by selling the contract to Pittsburgh. The contract showed that a $100,000 bonus doesn't mean the kid gets a cashier's check for $100,000 all at once. It read:

$ 5,200	to Pettit's father
10,000	advance to Stephani (repaid by Pirates)
1,500	to lawyers
50,000	at the rate of $5,000 a year for 10 years
18,000	at the rate of $6,000 a year for the first 3 years
10,000	home as a present
5,000	automobile as a present
750	for a honeymoon if he decided to get married
$ 100,450	Total

Salaries and Bonuses

He won one big-league game for the Pirates and got them a lot of publicity.

Established big-league players—especially those who never even smelled a dime bonus for signing and have made good—resent bonus babies. Especially those who just take up a seat in a major-league dugout and draw more money than they do. You can't blame them, either. I know that if I were hitting .400 and a high-school kid got a bigger salary I'd raise hell.

It's hard to tell what big leaguers are actually thinking, but the Boston Braves incident with Johnny Antonelli in 1948 was common knowledge among ballplayers. The Braves were fighting for their first pennant in history, when suddenly they read in the newspaper that the front office had given a bonus of approximately $65,000 to Antonelli. Then the club had to send an established big leaguer to the minor leagues to make room for him.

There was a lot of griping, I understand, and Johnny Sain really did more cussing than anybody. Johnny is usually pretty quiet, but he had a legitimate gripe. He had won 20 games the previous 2 seasons and was pitching the Braves to the pennant (they won the pennant and Sain won 24 games) and he wasn't getting anything close to what Antonelli was reportedly signed for.

Antonelli really started the trend in bonus players. He was coached by his father and looked like a polished player when he was eighteen. Actually you could almost call his bonus peanuts compared with what some of the kids are receiving today. Within a two-week period during the 1961 summer, big-league clubs spent over $4,000,000 on bonus players.

My War with Baseball

The highest individual bonus, which supposedly set the record, was the $175,000 the Pittsburgh Pirates announced they gave to Bob Bailey, an eighteen-year-old high-school infielder from Long Beach, California. The funny thing about it was Bailey's reason for signing with Pittsburgh. "Money wasn't the primary factor," he said. He was sent to Asheville, North Carolina, and I wouldn't be afraid to bet that he got all the razzing big-bonus players get in the minor leagues. Like "Hey, Brinks," "Moneybags" and "Fort Knox," etc. Sometimes this worries kids; sometimes it doesn't. It didn't bother Carl Yastrzemski, a kid who got over $100,000 for being a Little League, Pony League and Babe Ruth League star around Bridgehampton, Long Island. He hit .377 in his first professional season at Raleigh and hit .339 the next year at Minneapolis, which was in the American Association. So when he went to spring training with the Red Sox in 1961 everybody expected him to be the new Ted Williams. Even Ted said, "The kid has a good eye, is smooth, hits nothing but clothesliners, and will bat .320 his first year."

Despite the fact that Yastrzemski was playing left field—the position that Williams handled OK. for 17 years—he did put a little more pressure on himself by talking about his bonus. "The newspapers said I got a hundred thousand dollars," Carl said, "and I got every bit of that. They weren't exaggerating."

He didn't set the world on fire in his first season with the Red Sox, but there is still the possibility that he will eventually make good. It takes time to develop into a good player, and most bonus babies are rushed too fast.

Take the case of a major-league pitcher. When I was with the St. Louis Browns in 1952, we liked a high-school

Salaries and Bonuses

pitcher from St. Louis who worked out with us named Frank Baumann. But he had a fancy reputation and there wasn't any sense in the Browns talking to him. They didn't have any money and Baumann was talking big money. So the Red Sox gave him a contract of $85,000, which was spread over 5 years, sent him to Louisville of the American Association for a dozen games, then thought he was a big-league pitcher. He was sort of like a high jumper who tried the six-foot bar before he was ready for the five-foot-eight bar and lost confidence because he didn't make it.

But Bill Veeck, who was president of the Browns then and who wanted Baumann, eventually got him for practically a song when he (Veeck) was president of the White Sox in 1960. Baumann had matured and had the necessary experience by then. He never won as many as 5 games in any of his 5 seasons With the Red Sox, but won 13 games and led the American League in earned run averages in his first year with the White Sox. He had more determination than most bonus kids—they usually give up easier.

If an eighteen-year-old boy who has never been inside a big-league park but has a fast ball and curve can convince a major-league club that he is worth a big bonus, I recommend that he take it. I recommend that the kid get every cent he can. It's going to be a lot easier to get it before than after, because in my opinion most bonus players turn out to be flops anyway.

I think, though, that the practice of these big bonuses is outrageous. I don't believe any youngster is worth $100,000 unless he can play regularly for a big-league club the day he signs that contract.

My War with Baseball

I've come out strongly against the bonus before, and I don't think it has built up my popularity any. When I was working as a coach for the Chicago Cubs—I'm not any more—they called a meeting to talk about signing Dave Nicholson, a high-school outfielder who played in the same amateur league around St. Louis as Baumann and catcher Bob Taylor (Taylor got a $108,000 bonus from the Milwaukee Braves). Phil Wrigley, president of the Cubs, Manager Bob Scheffing, General Manager John Holland, Charlie Grimm, who'd been fired a couple of times previously (and once later) as manager, and Vice-President Pants Rowland and I were at the meeting.

"I haven't seen the kid play," I said, "but I don't think we should go a hundred thousand dollars, like you say we'll have to pay to get him. Unless he could play regularly tomorrow. You know how good an outfield you can buy for that? A lot better than the ones we've got now, and they're playing regularly."

It's obvious they didn't want my opinion. They didn't sign Nicholson, but they later signed Danny Murphy for $125,000—or that's what the papers reported—and I'm not working for them anymore.

A few bonuses won't get the Cubs out of the second division, in my opinion. Between the 1960 and 1961 seasons the newspapers carried a story that the Milwaukee Braves offered five darn good players and a big chunk of money to the Cubs for shortstop Ernie Banks. I would have made the deal. When you're trying to build a pennant contender out of a last- or seventh-place team, no one individual—Banks or Mantle—can make a club. Over the long haul a team will win more games with a balanced club rather than with a club with a couple of stars. All of the players reportedly offered in the deal could

Salaries and Bonuses

have played regularly for the Cubs. What's more, Banks' best years were behind him.

Even if Banks had been at his peak nobody can take a thirty-one-year-old star like him and start building a club around him. By the time you've built anything to beat anybody the star is too old and you're weak in the one spot where you were once strong. A pennant contender would be foolish to trade anyone of the caliber of Banks.

Practically the same thing happened to me in 1928. I was playing for the Boston Braves and became the playing manager in the last few weeks of the season when the club was in seventh place. We also had a very bad year at the gate. I really enjoyed playing for the Braves because the owner, Judge Emil Fuchs, was one of the nicest men I've ever met. When he told me that he had been offered 5 players and nearly $250,000 for me by the Chicago Cubs I strongly advised him to take it. "Look, judge Fuchs," I said, "I can only play one position and those guys can play five a lot better than any five guys you have now. They can help the team more in the long run than me. Besides, you can get enough money to bail yourself out for a while."

I hated to leave the Braves, and feel Fuchs hated to trade me, but in November I went to the Cubs. The Braves got the check from the Cubs, plus pitchers Percy Jones, Bruce Cunningham, Harry Siebold, catcher Doc Leggett and infielder Fred Maguire.

The success of building a team with young players doesn't always depend on the boys the scouts persuade a team to sign. It's the players that the scouts tout a team off of, which keep the club from blowing all its money on kids who haven't got the ability or determination to play big-league ball.

That's the reason for the Yankee success. Three of their scouts, Joe Devine, Bill Essick and Paul Krichell, were in a class by themselves. Particularly with all the money they had to spend. They signed the best players everywhere and stayed away from the bad ones. There are a few fellows on the Yankees today by the name of Mantle, Ford, Berra and Maris, who didn't get bonuses and aren't doing too bad.

But those scouts have all died within the last 8 years and the Yankees have been having trouble getting the cream of the player crop. The tip-off to this was in March of 1959 when Manager Casey Stengel suddenly found out he lacked the usual 2 or 3 outstanding rookies who were making some of the established regulars hustle. Instead of some fresh blood, he found himself watching such old fellows as Enos Slaughter, Virgil Trucks and Bobby Shantz—all fine ballplayers, mind you—who probably wouldn't have been in a Yankee uniform if the farm system had been producing like it had in the past. And after the 1959 season there was an awful lot of asking of "What's wrong with the Yankees?"

Even Ralph Houk, who took over for Casey Stengel at the end of the 1960 season, realized that there was a shortage of young players in the Yankee farms; and the Yankees went stronger on bonuses than they normally do in the spring of 1961. "I agree the bonuses are getting out of hand," Houk said, "but when you run out of kids you've got to buy them. Or maybe I should say, bid on them."

Salaries and Bonuses

The Baltimore Orioles are a perfect example of the fact that big bonuses won't buy a pennant. When I managed the Browns—who were transferred to Baltimore in 1953 and became the Orioles—I realized the team needed a complete rebuilding to ever knock heads with anybody for a pennant. This has to take time.

But the new Orioles' owners had plenty of money and they signed everybody who even looked like a major-league prospect. This meant kids who had a smart father or adviser who made the Orioles keep bidding to get them. They went to $40,000 for outfielder Jim Pyburn, $40,000 each for catcher Tommy Gastall and outfielder Bob Nelson, and $30,000 for Wayne Causey.

They really got burned badly on two prospects. All 16 teams were after Bruce Swango, a high-school pitcher from Welch, Oklahoma. Baltimore got him—for $36,000—and they also got a sore arm. When his sore arm improved, Swango said he didn't want to test his arm in front of a crowd. So the Orioles released him within a few weeks after the signing and without his so much as having thrown a hard pitch. While the scouts were in Oklahoma they got hot on Tom Borland, a pitcher from Oklahoma A and M, but Commissioner Ford Frick said there were "irregularities" in the deal and that the Orioles had to pay Borland the $40,000, although they never got him in uniform.

Despite the fact of getting no place with bonus babies, the Orioles went hog wild again in 1957 and signed outfielder Dave Nicholson ($110,000), catcher Frank Zup ($24,000) and pitcher John Papa ($50,000). Any Oriole fan can tell you that none of these kids has ever played $500 worth of major-league baseball in Baltimore. But the front office is still going for them. "There's only one

My War with Baseball

way to build a club," says the president of the Orioles. "That's to get the best young players available, and we're doing this as long as our money holds out."

Ironically, while the Orioles were outbidding most teams for the big-name kids, they lost so often that many players joked that they were almost ashamed to admit they were on the team. Then in 1960, practically overnight, they jumped from sixth to second place and battled the pennant-winning Yankees head and head for 140 games. Rookies were responsible for this—but none of the rookies were the bonus stars. The best of the bunch was shortstop Ron Hansen, the American League Rookie of the Year, who signed for $4,000. "And don't get me wrong," Hansen says, "that wasn't any bonus. That was my full salary for the first year. When I finished high school I had been reading about those 'untried kids' getting fifty- and eighty-thousand-dollar bonuses just to sign, and decided that's what I wanted—a big bonus. All the clubs except the Cubs and Giants talked to me—but quit talking when I started talking about a bonus."

When you compare Hansen—a non-bonus player starring for the Orioles—and Nicholson—a $110,000-bonus player now playing in the minor leagues—you wonder what makes a kid worth a big bonus.

When you scout a potential player you hope he has heart, then judge him on five things: (1) Can he hit? (2) Can he field? (3) Can he throw? (4) Can he run? (5) Does he have power?

Del Wilbur was scouting Nicholson in the same kid league in St. Louis that Bob Taylor (a catcher who got a $108,000 bonus from the Braves) and Baumann played in. Nicholson hit only .354 the last year he went to high

Salaries and Bonuses

school and batted only .260 in the Missouri Illinois Amateur League.

Wilbur filled out his report on Nicholson this way:

Hitting—Good

Throwing—good to excellent

Running—good to excellent

Fielding—good

Power—excellent

All the other clubs had scouting reports about the same, and they also took into consideration that Nicholson was six foot three, weighed 210 pounds and had a bull neck like Mickey Mantle.

Everybody needs another Mantle.

8. We Sold You

I'VE been asked to tell why baseball players are traded, how a player feels when he is traded or released, and how it feels to be fired as a manager. I'm the right man to tell about it—I've probably been fired more than any manager in history. I should be able to hold my own on trades. When I was still winning batting championships and managing a team to the World Series championship, I played on 4 different teams in 4 years from 1926 to 1929—the St. Louis Cardinals, New York Giants, Boston Braves and Chicago Cubs. I ended up as the manager, either for a full season or a few days, on every one of these teams. Even traded myself once, you might say.

They've been trading things in this country ever since some settlers came over on a boat and got Manhattan Island for about $25 worth of trinkets from a bunch of Indians who were crazy about beads. Come to think of it, though, those Indians haven't made any worse deals than some of those pulled in trading players.

Frank Lane took over as general manager of the Cleveland Indians in November, 1957, and when he left to go to the Kansas City Athletics in 1961 there wasn't a single player on the 1961 Indians roster that was on the team that Lane inherited. The Cleveland fans never got a chance to know the players—*Lane traded the entire team in three years.*

When you analyze some of the baseball deals a few years later you wonder how grown men who supposedly know all about baseball can make such trades. But outside of the few who trade just to have something to do in the front office, trades are generally made for definite reasons:

1. To try to strengthen the team at one or more positions and not weaken it by giving up the players it takes to get those who are needed.

2. To get new, fresh blood for drawing power when a regular player has worn out his welcome with the fans.

3. To replace a player who isn't playing regularly—and probably won't be due to circumstances on the team—and who demands to be traded.

4. To replace a player who is bad for a team's morale.

5. To sacrifice one high-priced star for 4 or 5 players who could play regularly, and who would help build up the team.

6. To unload a star who is over the hill by trading or selling him before he is completely washed up.

7. To unload a player the manager, general manager or owner just doesn't like—for personal reasons or for something he does on the field—just to get rid of him [like Sam Breadon of the Cardinals did to me in 1926 after once turning down the offer of $250,000 for me].

8. To put a star who is definitely finished on the waiver in the hopes that some other club will claim him

Trading and firing—two hazards of the world's most treacherous profession.

My War with Baseball

and pay his high salary—or just to get a younger player to replace him.

This last reason helped me make the best deal of my life. In June of 1926, Joe McCarthy, manager of the Chicago Cubs, thought that Grover Cleveland Alexander was dissipated, drank too much, and was finished as a major-league pitcher. Then too, Alex had suffered a broken ankle in spring training. They say that McCarthy and Alexander didn't like each other. McCarthy liked to tell Alexander how to pitch to certain batters, and Alex didn't want anybody to tell him how to pitch. The big blowup came in Pittsburgh when the Cubs were talking about how they were going to pitch to the Pirate batters. They brought up the fact that the Pirates' Rabbit Maranville had been traded away by the Cubs.

"We'll have to switch signs whenever he gets on second base," McCarthy said. "He's smart enough to remember signals from last year."

"Well, now," Alexander said, and sort of grinned, "if we thought there was much chance of this guy gettin' on second base we wouldn't have got rid of him, would we?"

The Cubs moved on to Philadelphia, and Alexander was finished with them. He had been put on the waiver list.

His wife, Aimée Alexander, said this was the toughest period of her husband's life. "He couldn't even talk about it," she said. "Tears would just come to his eyes. He thought he was finished in baseball forever and he loved baseball."

Even though Alex—that's what I always called him, though his nickname was Pete—had been in a

We Sold You

sanitarium at Dwight, Illinois, the winter before to try to quit drinking, I knew he still had a fast ball. Even if it was only half as good as it once was, it still was good. He had the greatest control I've ever seen. Could almost nick the corners of a soft-drink bottle cap. He won 30 games a season for 3 straight years while pitching for the Philadelphia Phillies in the smallest park in the big leagues. In one season he pitched 4 one-hit games. He once pitched 4 consecutive shutouts, including 16 in one season; twice he won 2 games in one day.

I was playing manager of the Cardinals, so I asked Branch Rickey, who was the general manager and had been the manager before me, to claim Alexander. I had heard of all those newspaper stories about Alex—that he carried a gin bottle more often than his glove—but I wanted him on my team. The Cardinals were in fourth place at that time, so that meant the 4 teams under us in the standings got a chance to pick him up for the $4,000 waiver price before we got to him. All 4 teams figured he was washed up, or figured something, because none of them took him. We got him on June 22.

All I said to Alexander when he reported was, "Glad to have you on the team. Think you can help us. Just follow the curfew like the other guys."

The next Sunday we played the Cubs, the team that had released Alexander. I don't think he ever pitched a better game in his life. He beat the Cubs, 3-2, in 10 innings and only gave up 4 hits. After the game he sort of tipped his cap, which was always too small for him, when he passed by McCarthy.

I knew Alex liked his highballs. He liked to go out and drink with his friends, and he had a lot of friends. But he never showed up drunk, and I don't think we could have won the National League pennant that year without him. It's obvious that he won the World Series for us. That's the series that went to 7 games, and Alex won 2, didn't lose any, and saved the last one for us. Next year, 1927, when I was with the Giants, I batted against Alexander and he was plenty tough. He won 21 games for the Cardinals, which certainly didn't look like he was finished as a pitcher, by any means.

Then there's the case where players are good but not quite as good as others on the team. They want to be traded. When I took over as manager of the Cincinnati Reds in the middle of the 1952 season they had two long-ball-hitting first basemen, Ted Kluszewski and Joe Adcock. Kluszewski had been hitting the hell out of the ball and was probably the top-power hitter in baseball at the time. Naturally he was the regular first baseman. Adcock had power, too. He knew it. I knew it. I couldn't play Joe at first—Klu was there—so I played him in the outfield to take advantage of his power.

Joe evidently didn't like the outfield and wanted to be the first baseman. He asked to be traded. Here's the story that one of my catchers, Dixie Howell, tells and he's better qualified to tell it than anybody because his locker was right next to Adcock's:

"It seemed that Joe would fall on his face every other day. Since my locker was next to his, all I'd hear was him griping. One day he came in raising hell about the Reds putting a big-hitting first baseman out chasing fly balls over an obstacle course. It got a little monotonous hearing the same thing every day, so I stopped him and said, 'Joe, look out the window. Over there is the head man's office. Why don't you either go raise hell with him or shut up? I'm struggling to hang on with the club myself!' Adcock looked like a mad bull when he stormed out of the clubhouse. He said he was going to insist that Hornsby either play him at first or trade him. I saw Adcock cleaning out his locker one day. 'Well, Dixie,' he said, 'you got me traded to the Braves.' "

I respected Adcock's desire to play. Can't blame him. He did all right at first base with the Braves, too. In 1953, the year after we traded him, he hit 33 homes runs and had a .285 batting average. The next year (1954) he hit 27 home runs and had a .308 batting average. In 1955 he hit 15 home runs and batted .264 and probably would have done better if he hadn't got hurt. But in the same 3 seasons Kluszewski hit 40 home runs and had a .316 batting average; hit 49 home runs and had a .326 batting average; and hit 37 home runs and had a .314 batting average.

Gabe Paul, who then was the general manager of the Reds, knows how to work with managers, and he and I pulled some good trades together. He once told me that Branch Rickey, general manager of the Brooklyn Dodgers, wanted to trade real bad for Cal Abrams, one of our outfielders. I didn't think Abrams would ever be anything great as a player, and told Paul that I thought it would be a good deal if we could get rid of Abrams for a solid player. We gave the Dodgers Abrams, threw in Gail Henley and Joe Rossi, and we got Gus Bell. Bell has been a big hero in Cincinnati ever since and the three players we gave up aren't even around the major-league parks any more.

Then there are cases where a club just wants to unload a player. Late in the 1949 season catcher Joe Tipton of the Chicago White Sox was a little late during one of the rare nights somebody checked to see that everybody was in bed. That put Tipton in the club's doghouse, and since he wasn't threatening for the batting championship (his average was .205) he was a marked man. So a week after the World Series the White Sox got rid of Tipton. The Philadelphia Athletics took Tipton and gave the White Sox a scrawny little second baseman named Nelson Fox. Nellie has had a .298 career batting average since then and exactly ten years after the trade, was named the American League's Most Valuable Player. You hardly saw Tipton's name in the box scores afterward.

The White Sox, who made some other outstanding trades—like getting Billy Pierce for Aaron Robinson—also are a good example of a team that was traded on a gamble and lost. After the White Sox won the pennant in 1959, their first in 40 years, they went after 2 straight in 1960, instead of building for the long-range future. They traded tomorrow for today, and in doing so had everybody in the barbershops, subways, and restaurants asking, "What about the Sox's future? All the young guys are gone."

Today the trade almost looks worse than the Fox deal in reverse. Bill Veeck sent third baseman Bubba Phillips, first baseman Norm Cash, and catcher John Romano to Cleveland for outfielder Minnie Minoso, catcher Dick Brown, and pitchers Don Ferrarese and Jake Striker. Outside of Minoso, whose baseball is behind him, the players Chicago got aren't even around the park. Cash, who has since been traded to Detroit, won the 1961 American League batting championship; Romano is one of the top catchers in the American League, and the White Sox are weak in catching now.

We Sold You

But the White Sox, playing for 1960, made good trades.

Romano would have had to play behind catcher Sherm Lollar, Manager Al Lopez said, and Cash had his chance in spring training and in most of the 1959 season and didn't make it. Cash didn't set the world on fire in 1960, either. I'm sure that if anybody with any say-so on the White Sox had figured Cash would hit as high as he did they wouldn't have traded him.

The same goes for the biggest star in the American League today, Roger Maris. He was signed out of high school by the Cleveland Indians in 1953, and the Indians—or at least General Manager Frank Lane—thought he didn't have the stuff. On June 14., 1958—which happened to be the trading deadline—Lane sent Maris, pitcher Dick Tomanek, and first baseman Preston Ward to Kansas City for Vic Power and Woody Held. It didn't look like such a bad deal—Held and Power played regularly for the Indians and did a good job. Maris hit only .240 for the entire season.

The following year, 1959, Maris raised his batting average to a .273 and hit 16 home runs, which isn't anything to get excited about. He figured Kansas City would be home, so he and his wife bought a home there (where they still live). The Athletics and Yankees, though, were making all kinds of deals then, and Maris got involved in one of those 3-Athletics-for-4-Yankees deals in December. Funny thing was that the late owner of the Athletics, Arnold Johnson, didn't want to trade Maris to the Yankees, and he and the Pirates were all set to trade him for shortstop Dick Groat. But General Manager Joe Brown and Manager Danny Murtaugh of the Pirates, who were discussing the swap in Johnson's hotel room in the

My War with Baseball

Fontainbleau in Miami, stepped out in the hall to ask each other a couple of questions. They decided to back out of the trade. Then Maris went to the Yankees, and of course was the American League's 1960 Most Valuable Player, and Groat was the National League's MVP. Maris is still young and he could be the biggest bargain in the history of baseball.

Many young players who aren't doing particularly well with one team, like in Adcock's case, certainly want to be traded. You always have the feeling you'll do better with another team; just like people always think another company will be better to work for. The time when it really hurts to be traded is when you've been a big star or even just a regular for a long period on one team. You usually own a home, your wife has it fixed up, the children like school and the kids around them. Then you get the phone call—right out of the night—that you've been sold and are supposed to report to this new team the day after tomorrow.

Richie Ashburn, whom I know from my coaching days with the Cubs, is a good example. He broke into the major leagues in 1948 with the Philadelphia Phillies, won 2 batting championships, and figured he had 3 or 4 more years left in the majors around 1960. Then he got that call one winter night. "You've been traded to the Cubs."

I know exactly how this feels. I loved St. Louis, had a house there and everything. Planned to spend the rest of my life there. Being the second largest stockholder in the Cardinals, I felt fairly secure. I had won 6 straight batting championships and managed the team to the pennant and World Series championships. Then 5 days before Christmas, 1926, the phone rang. It was the traveling secretary of the Cardinals. "We've traded you to the New

We Sold You

York Giants," he said. The owner—the guy who traded me because I had stood up for my decisions—didn't have the nerve to call.

It was no surprise to me when the Giants traded me to the Braves a year later. I had taken up for my players, and in doing so made the traveling secretary mad. He was the owner's best friend. The next year, when I went from the Braves to the Cubs, I suggested the trade to the owner myself so that he could make enough money to bail himself out of debt.

9. You've Got to "Cheat" to Win

WHEN Al Worthington quit the Chicago White Sox during the 1960 season and went home to Alabama most of the newspapers said it was over a salary argument. It wasn't. In my opinion he was a baseball misfit. Hell, he didn't like cheating.

If what Worthington claims is true, then he didn't come to the big leagues to play ball. What I call "cheating" here is nothing but outsmarting the opponent and it is part of the game. I've "cheated" or watched someone on my team "cheat" in practically every game. Ballplayers are always trying to beat the rules. If a big-league player doesn't like cutting the corners or playing with "cheaters," then he's as much out of place as a missionary in Russia.

Worthington's ethics are wonderful for a game between the Humane Society and Salvation Army. But not in the majors. He was a relief pitcher and not too good at it. But the White Sox were afraid some of their old pitchers might bum themselves up, and they got Worthington out of the minor leagues to sit in the bullpen just in case.

Al spent only six days in that centerfield bullpen in front of the new exploding scoreboard. And what do you suppose he discovered? Why, his team, the White Sox, had a spy inside that scoreboard who used high-powered binoculars to steal the opposing catcher's signals on every pitch. Then he'd flash a little red light in the right-hand corner of the scoreboard to let the Chicago hitter know whether the pitch was to be a fast ball, curve or whatever. "Baseball is a wonderful game," Worthington said later. "When it's not played on the up and up, it's time to quit. A coach picking up signs is part of the game. But not this other."

The PTA would go for that, too. But enforce rules against stealing signals in the big leagues and you wouldn't have enough guys left to play pitch and catch.

If Worthington had stayed around longer he could have made some other startling discoveries. That isn't the only way the White Sox cheat. Take, for example, the way they have their infield rigged. In Nellie Fox and Luis Aparicio they have the best pair of bunters in the game. Their specialty is bunting down the base lines. Most third basemen, unless they're dead certain they have the batter out, try to let the ball roll—and pray it rolls foul. But any time Fox or Aparicio lays one down in the home park it's got a damn good chance of staying fair. The reason is simple. The Sox have that foul line nicely banked up to keep bunts from rolling out.

Legal? Well, let me quote you Rule No. 104 in the rule book: "The infield shall be graded so that the base lines and home plate are level, with a gradual slope from the base lines *up* to the pitcher's plate."

The White Sox infield slopes, all right—in the opposite direction.

Some tricks of the game

Of course visiting teams could take advantage of the slanted foul lines, but again, laying down a safe bunt requires as much skill as getting a single into center field. Nobody has the bunters to match the White Sox.

Everybody rigs their park to suit their personnel. When Bill Veeck was president of the Cleveland Indians he even went so far as to move the fence in or out before each series, depending on whether or not the opposing club was a long-ball-hitting team. They had to pass a special rule to stop this.

But I don't blame him or anybody. If I was managing the White Sox I'd tilt those lines, too. In fact I would have tried to get the Cincinnati Reds to use the same trick when I was managing them in 1953, but they were so home-run happy they thought it was a disgrace to bunt.

Now take this "shady" business of stealing catchers' signs from centerfield. There isn't exactly any written rule against it, but if it wasn't cheating, guys wouldn't have to hide. Give the binoculars to the centerfielders. Still I can't see why anyone would get all excited about that. Cheating started when they threw out the first ball in the first game ever played and it's been going on ever since.

Every team with a scoreboard in centerfield—and that includes most all teams today—has a spy hidden inside at one time or another. I have. It's simple. You have to take down a sign for the inning score, and there's always a hole for the spy to peep out. There are always a few of the letter "O's" for the scoreless innings. The center of the "O" will open. When it's open, that's a fast ball; closed is a curve; and half open is a change-up. Or at

You've Got to "Cheat" to Win

least that's the way most teams have been doing it for years.

Teams try anything to get signals. In the old Detroit park there used to be a sign with an Indian on it, advertising Uneeda Water. The Indian had moving eyes. When the eyes moved sideways it meant the pitch was a curve; when they moved down that meant a change-up; and when they remained still that was the signal for a fast ball. There wasn't anything you could do about it—there isn't any rule in the book that bars Indian signs with moving eyes.

Here's a more recent example. The 1959 San Francisco Giants screamed bloody murder against the Chicago Cubs, the team I was working with then. Bill Rigney, the Giants' manager, claimed the Cub dugout was built on an unusually low level and that Al Dark, who was leaning down low on the steps, was stealing signals. This is impossible to do. But the main reason that Rigney griped so much was that he and Dark were once teammates and Dark had said that he and Rigney used to steal signs together. Actually, Dark was only a decoy—the Cubs had a man hidden somewhere else who was robbing the Giants of their signals.

Of course the Cubs had to change their tactics against the Giants later. Dark, the man who was supposed to be, and at times was, stealing their signals, became the Giants' manager.

Dark is a good example of the caliber of men who become managers. He was always accused of stealing signals, robbing the opposing team and things like that. And San Francisco couldn't wait to hire him as manager. He made a good manager, too, because he didn't cry about the other teams cheating him. He's just thinking up different ways to rob the Cubs, Phillies and the Braves—the last three teams he played for.

The Braves played 11 games, like all the other visiting clubs in Wrigley Field, and didn't open their mouths about the dugout or stolen signals. They thought their cheating method was better. And foolproof. Cubs' pitcher Bob Anderson was sitting in the Wrigley Field bullpen when he saw two guys in the bleachers carrying binoculars and waving scorecards like railroad flagmen. Despite their yellow golf hats and loud sport shirts, Anderson easily figured out who they were-pitchers Bob Buhl and Joey Jay of the opposing Milwaukee Braves. And Anderson knew damn well they weren't sitting out there because the tickets were cheaper. By the time manager Lou Boudreau got wind of the scheme and sent trainer Al Scheuneman to investigate, the two "Milwaukee fans" were walking away. They took a round-about way—but ended up in the Braves' clubhouse.

Boudreau took it all in stride. Afterward he leaned his foot on the bench in front of his locker and said, "Every club has done it at one time or another. When I managed the Indians we had somebody with glasses inside our scoreboard."

After all, when Boudreau was shortstop for the Indians they used to leave the grass in front of him longer than the rest of the field because he was a little slow and the long grass slowed down the ball.

I thought the sign-stealing deal was a mistake on the Braves' part. Not using a spy to steal signals, but using inexperienced men like Buhl and Jay. This kind of thing is an art, and Milwaukee coach Whit Wyatt—a fellow I've

You've Got to "Cheat" to Win

known for years—is regarded as one of the best. They should have let him handle important assignments like that.

All big-league teams are pulling the same stunt and working hard to improve it. It struck me kind of funny when Charles Finley bought the Kansas City Athletics and announced, the first thing, that he wanted a flashing scoreboard like the one in Comiskey Park. "That should pep up the fans," he said. What he really meant, I would say, was that it was being built to pep up his last-place A's. An electric scoreboard with those fancy blinking lights is the easiest way to transmit stolen signals.

There are plenty of legitimate ways to steal signals; coaches and runners do it every day. But personally I think today's teams are putting entirely too much emphasis on sign stealing and not enough on learning how to hit. Many batters demand signals be stolen for them, and I guess you can't blame them—they can't hit any other way. They used to try to steal signs for me, and I just said, "Thanks, keep the damn signs away."

Sign stealing is the cause of a good many bean balls. A guy can be batting, and the coach rubs his belt or something, meaning his team has stolen the signals and the next pitch will be a curve. So the batter gets braced for a curve—and the ball comes right for his head. He doesn't worry. The pitcher isn't going to fool him. The pitch is a curve and it's going to break and he'll knock it out of the park. But the other team isn't always idiotic. The signals have been switched and this particular pitch isn't a curve. It doesn't break and the only thing that's going to get knocked out is the batter.

My War with Baseball

When I started managing I always emphasized the fact that there is only a split second between the time somebody steals a signal and it's relayed to a coach who in turn relays it to the batter. Then if you have to change your stance the pitch is past you before you've changed. I always said, "Just watch the strike zone—and hit anything that's in it." That's all I ever did. George Sisler, Ty Cobb and lots of great hitters felt the same way. Going up to the plate with the notion that somebody is going to steal the signal and give you the pitch is guess hitting, and most guess hitters aren't worth an old broken bat.

When I was managing the 1952 Browns and 1953 Reds I had batters who sometimes looked like scrubwomen swinging brooms. Sometimes they wouldn't even swing at good pitches. Naturally I'd ask why. And one particular player—there were and still are many like him in the game—snapped, "I didn't get my pitch."

"Your pitch?" I growled back. "I thought you weren't a guess hitter."

So he says, "I'm not a guess hitter."

So I said, "Well then, you explain the difference to me between looking for a pitch and guess hitting."

To this day nobody has ever explained that to me.

To get back to cheating: Next to pitchers, infielders are the biggest cheaters. When I played second base I used to trip, kick, elbow or spike anybody I could. I didn't need to cheat when I was batting. Infielders like Eddie Stanky didn't have much ability, in my book, but still he was one of the best lead-off men of all time.

There's a rule against wearing ragged or slit shirt sleeves, but Stanky used to wear oversized sleeves

You've Got to "Cheat" to Win

starched stiff, and any time a pitch was fairly close he'd lean over and get nicked. Some of the teams raised holy hell, so the umpires stopped him. Next thing he was wearing big pants. Of course the umpire made Stanky change uniforms.

I think the best outsmarting infielder in the game today is Don Hoak of the Pirates. That's what makes him so valuable. His specialty is holding opposing runners by their belts when they try to take off from third base real fast.

I remember Hoak running that into the ground in 1950 when I was managing the Beaumont team in the Texas League. Hoak was playing third for Fort Worth and my players were raising hell about his holding their belts, blocking the base line, pinching them on the butts, and about every other dirty thing that's done. Well, Clint Courtney was on my team and he's just as mean as Hoak.

"Look," I told Clint, "if you make it to third base again and that little cheating S.O.B. touches you, let it go. Just lead off base enough to draw a throw from the catcher. Don't jump for the base. If you do I'll fine the hell out of you. Jump straight into that cocky little son of a gun's lap—with your spikes aimed right at his belly."

Our team was keyed up and looking for a good free-for-all. Each player picked out a man on the opposing team he wanted to stomp hell out of. Sure enough, Clint made it to third and right away Hoak started cheating and blocking his path. Clint did what I told him to do. It was the damndest fight I'd ever seen.

There are 20 teams in the big leagues and there must be about 25 catchers who've got more ability than Courtney. There probably are better catchers down in the bush

My War with Baseball

leagues. But Clint cashes a big-league pay check, and if I was managing again I'd sure as hell want him. He's so damn mean he reminds you of somebody who would run a torture camp for a hobby. He loves to tag runners in the head, and when he tags them right they have a headache worse than any moonshine hangover. We were having a practice game one day at Beaumont and Clint tagged his own teammate, Gil McDougald, so hard I thought Gil would have a concussion.

Hoak isn't the only big cheater. The White Sox have triple-threat cheaters. Take a 1960 Sunday game in Comiskey Park—where they have the scoreboard spy and banked base lines. The White Sox were leading Detroit by one run when Rocky Colavito of the Tigers hit such an easy pop fly to Nellie Fox, the Chicago second baseman, that Fox didn't have to move over three steps to catch it. Nellie is one of the best fielders in the business, but he dropped this pop-up. He created a force play at second base, putting out fast Al Kaline who had been on first, and leaving Colavito, a much slower runner, on first. It was a smart theft. That runner represented the tying run. There's a helluva lot of difference between cutting down a fast man and one who runs like he's pulling a trailer.

It is a violation of the rules to deliberately drop an infield fly ball to take advantage of a batter or runner. The umpire is supposed to nullify plays like that, but in this case he was watching something else and Fox cheated him. The Tigers argued, ranted and raved, but they had about as much chance as a fish out of water. Fox said he dropped the ball intentionally—after his team won the game by one run.

Of course Fox is on a perfect team for cheating. Bill Veeck, who was president of the White Sox at the time and has run the Indians and Browns, doesn't mind talking about the genial art of cheating. "Look," Veeck maintains, "we naturally tried to take advantage of everybody we could. When I was at Cleveland, Lou Boudreau, our shortstop, was pretty slow. We kept the grass in his area long. Joe Gordon was a ball of fire at second. Cut the grass short. Ken Keltner, our third baseman, was having leg trouble. We watered down his territory. We'd raise the mound for some pitchers—especially Bob Feller. We'd lower it for other guys."

Now it's no accident that the White Sox and Indians have the two best doctored diamonds in baseball—they have the best "riggers" doing it. You see, Emil Bossard, the head groundkeeper for the Indians, has three sons: Harold and Marshall, who work as his assistants; and Gene, who is employed by the White Sox. They're so valuable at rigging infields that the first thing Boudreau did when he was named manager of the Kansas City Athletics in 1955 was to try to hire one of the young Bossards as groundkeeper. He didn't look for players. He told Harold, the oldest son, "You can write your own ticket."

"When I was manager of the Indians," maintains Boudreau, "I wouldn't be a bit surprised if Emil didn't win as many as ten to twelve games a year for us. He was the tenth man in our line-up." And Lou meant it, too. The players thought so much of Emil's work that they voted him three-fourths of a World Series share in 1954, which amounted to $5,034.

Not only does Emil rig foul lines—tilt them like a saucer—but he speeds up or slows down fields, depending on the speed of a team that is coming in for a series. Now while the Pirates have their diamond concrete-hard—

and the Indians have had theirs the same way—Veeck claims they won the 1948 pennant by "slowing down."

One reason Emil has been so valuable at this kind of work, which he maintains is as legal as stolen bases, is because he doesn't publicize it. His son Gene is pretty proud—and outspoken—about his conniving for the White Sox. "We're a bunting club and build up the line higher than the grass beside it," Gene has said out loud in reference to the line that keeps many of Aparicio's and Fox's bunts from rolling out. "On other clubs, guys like Mantle, Maris or Skowron can't hurt you by bunting. Boy, if they bunt they're doing you a big favor."

Another thing Gene learned from his father and practices in Comiskey Park is to soften the area in front of home plate for a low-ball pitcher. That way, any time a ball is hit in the soft ground your infielders have more time to grab it. But he doesn't keep it a secret. "If a fastball pitcher was going," Gene says, "you'd expect him to get a couple of guys out on strikes, a couple more on flies to the outfield, walk one, and anything can happen on the other pitch. But with a guy like Bob Shaw, who's now with the Athletics, four out of the six guys are likely to hit on the ground. So we sure get out the water hose."

Actually there is no written rule against altering the grass, but that's pretty much like putting an air conditioner in your own dugout and a heater in the visitin team's for a Fourth of July double-header. Which isn't farfetched, either. Frank Lane, who had enough deals like this going for him at Cleveland, did it. "What's wrong?" Frank would ask. "Players can bring their own air conditioners. We don't search them."

You've Got to "Cheat" to Win

After Lane left Cleveland for the Kansas City Athletics he didn't even put a toilet in the visiting team's clubhouse. I guess he figures he gets an advantage out of making the opposing team's players 'walk practically across the field, embarrassed because everybody in the stands knows where they're going.

This sort of thing isn't illegal, but it's sure as hell illegal to fool around with that mound. The fourth rule in the book says a pitcher's mound must be 15 inches above the level of the diamond. And pitching is such a science that a 13- or 17-inch mound can wreck a pitcher's control. The plate is only 17 inches wide, and the sudden change in height can easily make 3 or 4 inches difference in where the ball goes. Most pitches are determined balls or strikes by a fraction of an inch anyway.

Changing the mound doesn't hurt a visiting pitcher who's aware of it, and it really helps a pitcher who has it tailor-made for him. I've had long-legged and long-armed pitchers who demanded the mound 2 or 3 inches higher than legal—so they could get more leverage when they came off the mound.

Pitchers like Bob Turley, Bob Friend, Don Drysdale and Sandy Koufax, Joey Jay, or most of the Yankee pitchers certainly would benefit from a higher mound—if they knew it. Little guys like Whitey Ford or Jim O'Toole would be hurt by it.

It's the same principle as in basketball, where the basket is supposed to be 15 feet from the free-throw line. If the distance is 16 or 17 feet and the player doesn't know about it, then his shots fall short and he can't figure out why. Wouldn't hurt, though, if a player knew and practiced against it. A couple of years ago visiting teams were murdered on free throws in Cincinnati Gardens. Finally one coach demanded the setup be measured. The distance was 17 feet.

Of course you can always blame things like that on the janitor. The groundkeeper can catch the blame—if it's necessary to raise hell—in baseball. Besides, how can a manager be accused—even if he actually orders the fields to be rigged? I never touched a shovel or pile of dirt in my life. Neither has any other big-league manager. It might seem puzzling why something isn't done about cheating. For one thing, ballplayers just don't tell on each other. They'll scream during a game when they're hot. But not later. When Dick Groat sat down to tell his collaborator the story of the Pirates' world championship, he stopped cold when he was merely asked about the batting weaknesses of Dale Long, an ex-Pirate who played for the Yankees in the World Series.

"That's where I absolutely draw a line," Groat insisted, "even with the other team. I don't want to be the guy to squeal on Long. He might do the same to me. We might be on the same team again."

That's the way players are. A player doesn't even tell his own manager—or roommate—how he cheats. All a manager cares about a pitcher is that he gets the side out; all he cares about the other players is that they get on base. He doesn't care *how* they do it, either.

They'll never stop cheating. Nobody wants to. And it doesn't pay to gripe. Look at Birdie Tebbetts. When he finished his project to prove Lew Burdette was throwing spitters, he was out as Cincinnati manager. His next job was executive vice-president of the Milwaukee Braves. His biggest winner? Lew Burdette. The more spitballs

Burdette throws, the more Tebbetts is willing to pay. Today Tebbetts is managing Burdette. It would be easier to find out who has the Greenlease ransom money than to prove a spitball charge.

Larceny in professional baseball begins right at dirt level. What's more, dirt is so important that most people insist dirt—and not Bill Mazeroski's home run—decided the 1960 World Series. Lots of ballplayers are still calling the Pittsburgh groundkeeper the "Most Valuable Pirate." Even claimed he deserved a full share of the series' money. I think he should get two shares. Ted Kluszewski, one of my old players and an ex-Pirate who is neutral in the argument, says a highway-construction crew couldn't get a harder infield than Forbes Field where the Pirates play ball.

Forbes Field was built back in 1909 and they've been rolling the infield ever since. Through the years most of their top hitters—Max Carey, Pie Traynor, Lloyd and Paul Waner—all hit down on the ball, and it was to Pittsburgh's advantage to have a rock-hard field that would cause a lot of so-called bad bounces.

When those guys retired, the Pirates played so lousy for years that nobody cared if they even had an infield. Four years ago, when it was clear that Pittsburgh finally had a team with a good shot at the pennant, visiting teams started raising hell about the concrete-hard infield.

The front office could have had the diamond plowed up and made as cushioned as Yankee Stadium or any park. But if the Pirates even considered having that infield softened they should have their heads examined. That would be sillier than giving away their star player.

My War with Baseball

Pittsburgh's line-up is filled with slashing-type hitters. Dick Groat, who had the highest average in the big leagues in 1960, got plenty of points from that infield. He's a right-handed hitter who hits to right field, which isn't what a big leaguer is supposed to do. But Groat slaps that ball into right field—right through that rock-like infield. Sometimes the ball shoots so crazy that you couldn't field it with a bushel basket. Most of the Pirates—Bill Virdon, Don Hoak, Roberto Clemente, Bob Skinner—have the same slashing hitting style.

Here's how valuable that infield is: In the eighth inning of the final 1960 World Series game the Yankees had the Pirates 7-4, and for all practical purposes had the world championship in the bag. Then Pittsburgh got a single through that infield, but the Yankees still figured it was all over. Bill Virdon, who hits a lot of ground balls, poked a grounder directly at shortstop Tony Kubek. All Tony had to do was make a simple pickup—like he had done thousands of times in the American League parks—and start the double play. But this was in Forbes Field. The ball never touched Kubek's glove. It bounced so sharply into Kubek's throat that doctors didn't know for a day if Tony would ever talk again.

The Pirates converted the break into 3 runs, and if it hadn't been for that brick infield, Mazeroski could have hit 2 home runs in the ninth and the Yankees would still have won the series. And don't think it's sour grapes on my part. I'm a National Leaguer and I was pulling for the Pirates.

Since all the rule book says about an infield is that it should be dirt, is the Pirate scheme illegal? Hell yes. That isn't any dirt infield. That's like concrete. But it's smart baseball.

You've Got to "Cheat" to Win

A lot of other teams have won world championships with this kind of cheating, including those baseball immortals in the Hall of Fame with me today. Connie Mack, who is supposed to be something of a baseball god, used to tip the hitter's bat with his oversized mitt when he was catching. When he was exposed he would keep the baseball the opponents were going to hit in the icebox overnight.

Take John McGraw, who managed the New York Giants for 30 years and was probably the smartest cheater of all time. Lots of pitchers used to use dirt to keep their hands from getting slippery. John doused the mound with liquid soap, and old-time pitchers are still wondering why their control was so damn lousy against McGraw's world-champion teams.

They had cheating down to a science back in 1898. Tommy Corcoran, shortstop captain of the Cincinnati Reds, was coaching at third base against the Phillies when his spikes got caught in what looked like a vine. He jerked it and several yards of wire popped out of the ground.

He called time. Then the umpires followed Corcoran as he traced the cable across right field to the Phillies' dressing room. Morgan Murphy, a second-string catcher, was sitting by a little peephole with a telegraph set and binoculars. Murphy was stealing the catcher's signals and using the Morse-code buzzer to transmit the signal to the third base coach. One buzz meant a fast ball, two buzzes was a curve, and three buzzes a slow ball or change-up. The third base coach relayed the signals to the batter.

That's part of baseball. The manager of the Phillies, George (Tweedy) Stallings, used tricks like these to convert some last-place clubs into World Series winners. He was also the manager of the Miracle Braves of 1914, who were dead last on July 4th and won the World Series in 4 straight games. And you have to say that tricks helped him. He took over the 1910 New York Yankees, then known as the Highlanders, and brought them from eighth place to second place.

His Highlanders got to guessing every pitch Detroit pitchers were throwing and the Tigers started investigating. Their trainer sneaked inside the scoreboard and found a little handle that allowed the "O" to be shifted around to signal the pitch. But the funny thing was the trick Stallings used to decoy the opposing team's attention from the scoreboard. There was an advertisement on the fence which featured a movable hat. The opposing team thought it had caught the hat as the signal—the hat moved left for a curve, right for a change-up, and remained still for a fast ball. And Detroit, the team that exposed Stalling's stunt, later got caught using that Indian advertisement sign with the moving eyes.

I was playing for the Cardinals against the Phillies in the same park, later known as Baker Field, in 1925 when somebody noticed a white towel being pulled in and out of the Phils' dressing-room window in centerfield. They had a spy with binoculars catching signals. Same deal. A stretched-out towel was the signal for a fast ball, no towel meant a curve, and a rolled-up towel was a change-up pitch. That didn't stop them, though. They just changed colors of the towels. A few years later, when all the players from that team retired, they told me how they did it. Pulled it on every team for a long time.

You've Got to "Cheat" to Win

So Worthington shouldn't have gotten all worked up over the White Sox using the electric scoreboard to cheat. The only thing new was the scoreboard.

10. Bean Balls and Spitters

I CAN conservatively say that 95 percent of the pitchers in baseball today throw any kind of pitches they can get away with. The other 5 percent aren't necessarily lily white: they just don't know how to throw illegal stuff. It takes years of practice and plotting to be an expert "cheater." So expert in some cases that even a player's own manager doesn't always know what happens. Besides, managers are hired and fired so often it's too dangerous for a pitcher to reveal any of his secrets.

Most catchers don't even know how a pitcher goes about cheating. On every club I've managed I've heard catchers holler, "What the hell was that pitch?" The catcher, in most instances, signaled for a curve and got one with fringe benefits—a good, hopped-up pitch. When I heard those catchers yell I wondered, too; but it wouldn't have done any good to ask what happened. Like all managers, I eventually lost my job and ended up on another club.

I can't remember half a dozen pitchers in my lifetime who wouldn't do anything to bail themselves out of a jam. I know I would if I was a pitcher. And pitchers who don't want to "cheat" to win just don't fit into a winning organization.

My War with Baseball

If a pitcher knows his arm isn't strong enough to fire an important strike past a hitter, or his control is gone, that doesn't leave him much choice. He's got to get the batter out. They don't pay ballplayers much money down in Knoxville or Raleigh. That's where the nice guys play. The smart pitchers—the pitchers who know how to cheat—draw the big money in Chicago, New York and Los Angeles.

Now old-fashioned umpires and purists are going to sneer at me, "You're popping off about spitballs and things like that. The spitball is a myth. They outlawed the spitter in 1920."

Yeah, I know they banned the spitter. It was too dangerous, they said. In fact, my older brother, Everett, scared more people with it than anybody. He and lots of other guys used to carry a pocket of slick-elm bark, chew it up and spread it on the ball. Not only would the ball do all kinds of tricks, but with that bark and spit flying off it the ball looked like a little bowl of slaw sailing toward the batter.

Banning the spitter and any kind of tampering with the ball doesn't mean pitchers have stopped doing illegal tricks with the ball, any more than prohibition stopped drinking. Why, I've managed pitchers who filed their thumbnails sharper than those super razor blades that ballplayers use on television. Any time they gave up a hit and the umpire didn't throw out the ball they had a chance at a perfect robbery. They'd whack the seams with that sharp nail and use the hole to make the ball hop, dart, and shoot in or out. It wrecked the hitter's timing—and hitting is 50 percent timing. That's what causes lots of those little dribblers and easy pop-ups.

Ninety-five percent of the pitchers in baseball today throw any kind of pitch they can get away with.

My War with Baseball

Even if the batter screams his head off—and lots of them do every season—it doesn't do any good. They can't prove a pitcher cut the ball. The reasoning is that the seams were cut accidentally. "I'll be darned," the pitcher or catcher frowns in all innocence, "guess that last base hit cut the ball, huh, Ump?" The umpire knows better, but what can he do? Are they still doing that today? Well, I'm not out on the mound, but pitchers still have thumbnails, don't they?

Pitchers who have perfected the fine art of cutting, nicking, or wetting the ball are twice as effective as other pitchers—and earn three times as much money. They deserve it, too. They're the big winners. They don't use the illegal stuff on every pitch. Just when they're in a tough spot. I'm not talking about the Little League or Ivy League, but the major leagues. It's a professional game for grown men and you only get paid for winning. To my knowledge nobody ever questioned anybody for his honesty before hiring him.

On the contrary, I always told my pitchers this: "It's you against the hitter. Those batters would hit you over the head if they could. Do anything you can to get them out. And if you don't you won't find me out on the mound patting you on the back real nice-like and waiting for the relief pitcher. If I have to come out you should be kicked in the ass."

Lots of pitchers will struggle along for a few years with 2-4, 4-5, or 6-8 records. They know what's next: the manager will shake their hands real nice and gentlemanly like and hand them their releases or tickets to the Piedmont League. But some of these guys, boom! Suddenly a pitcher has an 18-6 record and spends the winter going to banquets and telling people how he developed a

Bean Ball and Spitters

new pitch. "Our pitching coach showed me how to control my curve," he'll say piously, and hope some sportswriter is listening. Then the sportswriter will hack out corny stories about how "his new slider really gave him a winning assortment."

Slider, hell. A slider isn't anything more than a little dinky curve. Better call the guy a slipper. He's learned how to slip those balls past a hitter when he's in a jam. And if the pitching coach taught him anything, it was what I always hammered in my pitchers' heads: "Do anything you can get away with."

They did, too. I had one pitcher who would chew coffee grounds and drop a few of them in the seams. They could have stopped that by outlawing coffee. I didn't teach my pitchers this particular trick, but I certainly didn't mind them using it. We got paid to win.

I've also heard that a little Vaseline or baby oil strategically placed behind the ears or in the holes of a belt has gotten more than just one average pitcher out of trouble.

Some of my pitchers have robbed batters the same way. When I was playing manager of the St. Louis Cardinals in 1925-26, I'd walk in from second base to settle down a pitcher. Most times if I'd leave a pitcher in I'd know he would be O.K. Lots of my pitchers could strikeout guys if they were drunk.

If I left in Allen Sothoron, for example, I was certain he knew how to take care of himself. Allen had coarse sandpaper mounted inside his glove. Sometimes the paper would be sticking through the seams, another time it would be sticking through a hole in his glove. You couldn't see the paper. It was dyed to match the glove.

My War with Baseball

But you could see the ball rise, hop, and shoot every which way.

That's why batters always scream "spitball" and "wet one," and they'll go on yelling as long as they play baseball. But they can't prove a thing. They were screaming in 1932, 1942, 1952 and they're screaming now. They spend all season screaming at Lew Burdette of the Milwaukee Braves. Which is reasonable. In my opinion Lew has the very best spitball in baseball.

Burdette has a screwball which comes off the third finger instead of the first two fingers, and breaks down and in to right-handed hitters, and away to left-handed hitters. He uses the same wrist-snapping motion for his spitball—and gets all the benefits from it. Most of the time. When opposing benches have been yelling, "It's wet," at Burdette, they've been right.

Lew doesn't even try to deny he throws spitters. In fact, he wants the batter to think he uses a little water—even when he doesn't. Makes some hitters jittery. Hell, he keeps some teams excited all season. After he had won his first game in 1961, Lew had the St. Louis Cardinals so worked up that they were spending more time counting spitballs than batting. "Some of my guys counted at least nine spitballs," Solly Hemus, the Cardinals' manager, yelled, "but I say Burdette threw close to twenty—the most I've seen him use since I first saw him pitch.

"There's no sense filing a complaint about it," Hemus went on, "there's no teeth in the rule as it stands now. As long as they permit him [Burdette] to go to the mouth he'll throw spitters. The fact that he must go to the resin bag after going to the mouth doesn't mean a thing.

Anyone can palm the resin bag. There are more ways than one of skinning a cat. But I can't blame him. The umpires don't stop him and it's his best pitch."

A few years ago Burdette and Leo Durocher were waiting to go on Bob Hope's television program when Durocher asked Lew to show Hope how to throw a spitter. Burdette answered almost by reflex action, "See, I got heavy eyebrows and sweat a lot. Just touch my eyebrows, fix my cap, wipe my face, fumble with the resin bag, turn the ball in the glove like this . . . ah, hell, Leo, whatta you trying to do? You know you never saw me throwing a spitter . . . ha ha!"

"You mean," Durocher snapped, "I can't prove it."

There's no telling how many times I've heard umpires growl back at batters: "Look, bone dry. The same as it's been the last dozen times." But that's exactly what I would have to say if I was umpiring. What can an ump say? "Yes, he's throwing spitters, but I can't catch him." Hardly. An umpire has to alibi because he is in an impossible situation. The only way he can prove Burdette, Don Drysdale, Sam Jones, Early Wynn or anybody else throws a spitter is to catch him with spit on the ball. If the umpire starts to the mound the pitcher wipes off the ball. When a pitcher throws it to the catcher, the catcher nonchalantly brushes the ball against his uniform while he's bringing it out of his mitt, and the moisture is gone.

So why can't an umpire alibi? When an outfielder misses a fly ball he always tells his manager the sun got in his eyes.

Nobody else will ever prove a pitcher throws spitters. After Birdie Tebbetts followed me as manager of the Cincinnati Reds in 1954. he spent more time trying to pin a spitball rap on Burdette than he did managing. Tebbetts was convinced Lew used spitters. So he had a movie camera filming every action Lew made on the mound, and used up more film than Twentieth Century-Fox. What did it prove? That you can take motion pictures of baseball games.

I've always been partial to pitchers like Burdette. When I was trying to determine whether or not to take out a pitcher I'd say to myself, "What does this guy do in the clutch? Anything he can get away with. Fine." I always felt better about leaving him in if he was a "smart-money" pitcher. I couldn't risk my reputation and job on somebody with a scoutmaster's attitude.

I'm no different than today's big-league managers. I've either played, managed or coached with or against most managers and know how they look at a situation with a pitcher in a big jam. And since Don Drysdale of the Los Angeles Dodgers publicly admits he does *everything* to win, he certainly shouldn't mind if we use him as an example of how to shortchange the batter. If he has the bases loaded there's only one way Manager Walt Alston will look at it. "Does this guy come through? Does he have an out pitch?" If Alston knows his pitcher is a smart guy with the ball—like Drysdale claims he is—chances are he'll leave him in.

If Drysdale gets the side out without any more damage he will stay in and get a chance at the win. If somebody clobbers the ball he gets to take a nice shower and cuss up a storm in the clubhouse. That's a situation that will mean over $1,000 to Drysdale or any pitcher.

So a pitcher with any ambition or guts doesn't have much choice. Say he's been using the standard stuff—

Bean Ball and Spitters

curves, fast balls, and an occasional change-up. Then the last thing most batters will expect is something new. And you don't have to dip the ball in a bucket of water or spit on it to cheat the batter.

Here's what 95 percent of the smart pitchers will try to do: adjust their pants, cap, or something. Or rub their pants legs. That's legal. All pitchers rub their pants legs, and all of them use resin to keep their hands dry. Resin—which is a coarse powder—is legal. When the pitcher rubs the hard resin on his leg, then sweats a lot, he's got a helluva good way to get the batter out. Rub that ball on his leg and the wet, hard resin makes a spot on the ball. That's what guys call a "shine ball." It's illegal, but what pitcher cares? That shiny spot gives a batter a bad look at the ball.

Pitchers have other ways of robbing hitters. If they want a little help or spot on the ball, the catcher accidentally scrapes it against the rough hooks on his mitt. They'll do it plenty of times this year. Or when a catcher whips the ball around the infield one of the infielders will rough it up. How do I know? I used to rough the ball up—do anything I could—for lots of pitchers. Any kind of spot on the ball really gives the pitcher an advantage.

If a smart batter raises living hell and the umpire does find a little spot on the ball, all he can do is throw it out of the game. He can't walk to the mound and look behind the pitcher's ears. If guys weren't working over the balls you Wouldn't need very many. They used to open a game with a dozen balls. Today they open with 4 dozen. And those other 3 dozen aren't all knocked out of the park, either.

My War with Baseball

If anybody still doesn't believe me, ask Joe Gordon, who used to manage the Athletics. Back in the early part of the 1961 season, when the weather was still pretty cold, the Yankees were talking about the spitball. Whitey Ford had just shut out the Athletics, and his best pitch the whole game had been a sinker. "In the old days," Manager Ralph Houk was saying, "the spitter used to do all different things. But now they're just not loading it up so much. Mostly it just sinks."

"Not me," Ford said. "Throw the spitter out there today and it would have ice on it. It was so cold it'd stick to the catcher's hand."

Ford had been accused of throwing a spitter plenty of times, but he doesn't usually talk about it so frankly. But even though his team had just been shut out, Gordon didn't think there Was much he could do about it.

"I don't know if he's throwing the spitter," Gordon said, "but if he is, more power to him. That's the idea of the game, isn't it? To outsmart your opponent?"

Most times when a team hollers "Stick it in his ear" they aren't just exercising their tonsils. Everybody throws the brush-back pitch. It's also called a "duster," "bean ball," or "extra tight" pitch, depending on how good your vocabulary is. They've been throwing at batters ever since people started getting paid to win, and evidently they're doing more of it now than ever, because players are required to wear plastic helmets. I don't know if the helmets were installed to keep guys from getting hit, but they definitely encourage more of those "extra tight" pitches. Pitchers aren't worried about killing anyone now.

Bean Ball and Spitters

I'm not criticizing pitchers for using bean balls. Like Drysdale says, "We're paid to win." Pitchers don't throw at batters to fracture skulls or kill anybody; all they want to do is scare 'em to death. But just the same, let a baseball traveling at 95 miles an hour hit you in a particular spot and you go to the hospital while somebody runs for you. Batters are aware of that.

Some guys deny throwing dusters, of course, and others use them more than any other pitch. Lots of others are really proud of their dusters. Take Sal Maglie. "There are people who believe I threw at the heads of the Dodgers," Maglie says, "and they're a hundred percent correct. In fact, I couldn't have accomplished much as a pitcher without the knockdown pitch. My advice to pitchers is forget the fifty-dollar fine for knocking down hitters. This is the best pitch in baseball."

Then too, Early Wynn of the White Sox, who probably is the best at this in the American League, says, "The knockdown is as legal as Sunday school. When they outlaw batters hitting up the middle, I'll quit dusting people off."

There is that automatic $50 fine for deliberately throwing at a batter, but even the best umpire in baseball today, Jocko Conlan, knows the pitch is fairly well accepted. "Some umpires won't even try to enforce the rule against bean balls," Jocko will tell you. "They say it's impossible to tell the difference between a deliberate knockdown pitch and an unintentional wild pitch. In fact, there are more bean balls than ever these days." Jock ought to know, too. He was a pretty fair ballplayer in his day and one of his managers—George Stallings— used to stand up on the dugout steps and yell, "Hit 'em in the head. If you can't hit the head, hit the navel."

But, as the players know, it's such an accepted practice that most managers discuss how they're going to throw at guys before a game. I always did. If I was managing in the National League today, here's how I'd have my pitcher throw, say, at the Pittsburgh Pirates. Take Dick Smart, their power hitter. He wants an inside fast ball, or naturally, a fast one down the middle. He doesn't like an outside pitch. I would knock him down on the very first pitch. Throw right for the tips of his shoulders. When he got back up out of the dirt he'd be an inch or so farther away from the plate. Then the pitcher could concentrate on Stuart's weakness—the outside corner.

Now a duster would be excellent for Roberto Clemente. He loves to hit the first pitch. He also goes to the plate half scared. Sometimes he's ducking before they ever pitch to him. Think what happens to Clemente's confidence when he hears the opposing dugout yell "Flatten him" or "Stick it in his ear" and the pitch sails right toward him and he has to hit the dirt. He'll then be just half as effective.

Even though the Pirates won the 1960 World Series, Clemente spent half the winter talking about people throwing bean balls at him. "Why they pick on me?" he said everywhere he went. "I'm sick and tired of getting pitched at. We were behind ten-nothing in the World Series, and Whitey Ford brushed me back. Our pitchers should do the same to get even." This was six months after the Series, too, so there's no telling how excited he was when it happened. He won the 1961 batting championship, and there's no telling how good he could be if he wasn't scared.

Dusters have the same effect on lots of other hitters. The Pirates' batting coach, George Sisler, even maintains

Bean Ball and Spitters

that "any hitter scared of getting hit might as well quit." Dusters didn't scare Sisler either—he hit .422 one season.

It's funny, though, how ballplayers react to these "extra tight" pitches. Don Zimmer and Minnie Minoso, in particular, freeze when a pitch sails toward them. But still they're not afraid of the ball, no matter how many times they get hit. A duster wouldn't have any effect on Don Hoak of the Pirates. Brush him back and he'll be in the middle of the plate. It doesn't bother Pete Runnels, either, and everybody knows they are both good ballplayers. The same goes for other guys. They threw at Babe Ruth and Ty Cobb. They aimed at my head, too.

Sometimes a duster will just make a player try harder. They throw at Roger Maris and it doesn't help the pitcher. Maris hits more home runs than anybody. They throw at Dick Groat and he never gripes. Take the time the Pirates needed to whip the Milwaukee Braves to practically clinch the 1960 pennant. Groat saw Milwaukee's Eddie Mathews leaving a big hole down the third base line. He stepped out of the box and decided to poke one down the vacant line. Only Dick must have forgotten who was pitching—Lew Burdette. And Lew, as I've said, has a "jam" pitch and knows the only thing that counts is winning. Burdette came in with an inside fast ball and Groat got it right where he wears his watch. Instead of a cheap hit, Dick got a broken wrist. Since that pitch knocked out Groat, the team captain and league's leading hitter, at the most crucial time of the season, it wouldn't have been unreasonable to accuse Burdette of deliberately throwing at Groat. To my knowledge Groat never said a word. He's a professional and this is a professional game.

My War with Baseball

There are three kinds of dusters, in my opinion, and Groat got the one called the "tight" pitch. That's when the pitcher throws tight, in on the fists, trying for a strike. The others are the "brush-back," around the knees or shoulders, or the "deliberate knockdown," "duster," "bean ball" or whatever you want to call it.

Regardless of the rules or any additional rules that may be voted in, bean balls will continue. It's an important pitch; as Maglie says, it's even more important to have a "bean-ball reputation." Take Robin Roberts, a fine pitcher and one of the finest gentlemen you'll ever want to meet. He's such a nice guy that the batters know he doesn't throw—or at least hasn't been throwing—bean balls. So they take a firm stance and dig in, and the more any hitter is set and dug in with his spikes the better chance he has of knocking the ball out of the park. And Roberts has led the major leagues for years in giving up the most home-run balls.

But there aren't many guys around like Roberts. There also isn't much the batter can do to get even against bean balls unless he has Ty Cobb's nerve. Ty would drag a bunt to get the pitcher to cover first base, then step on the pitcher's feet with his spikes. And Cobb also had the sharpest spikes in baseball. But actually, I don't think there are a half-dozen guys today who would ever consider trying Ty's trick. It takes guts to pull this kind of revenge, because the player has to bat again and it isn't hard for a pitcher to hit a guy in the head. It's a lot easier when he tries.

11. Nobody Wins the World Series

MY biggest thrill in all baseball was making a simple tag on a runner trying to steal second base. The play was the biggest surprise of my career, and I'd have to say the biggest break any of my teams ever got. It also goes to prove that the World Series is not won—it's lost. The guy I tagged out—and by a mile, too—was Babe Ruth. Babe just decided to "take off" and he merely slid into my glove and tagged himself for the out that gave my St. Louis Cardinals the 1926 World Series championship over the New York Yankees. The Yankees were 15-to-1 favorites to beat us in the Series, too.

It was October 10, a Sunday, cold and drizzling in Yankee Stadium. So cold in fact, that only 38,093 persons turned out in New York for the seventh game of the Series. We had the Yankees 3-2 going into the seventh inning when we ran into trouble. Jesse Haines was my pitcher and going good. But he walked Earle Combs, and Mark Koenig sacrificed him to second. Then Ruth, who had hit a home run in the fourth inning, was up. I told Jesse to walk him. Bob Meusel forced Ruth at second and Combs went to third. Lou Gehrig, the "2" man in that famous "1-2 punch" of the Yankees, was up, and Haines walked Gehrig, too, loading the bases. Then

207

My War with Baseball

Jesse turned to me and sort of wiggled his hand. He had worn the skin off the index finger of his right hand throwing knuckle balls. He had to come out of the game. Willie Sherdel, a left-hander, was already warming up in the bullpen.

We didn't have any telephones to the bullpen like they do today. I just waved and motioned for the guy to come on in. I wanted Grover Cleveland Alexander, who was thirty-nine years old, had pitched and won a complete game the day before for us, and was a guy the Cubs decided was washed up and had released. Some people figured Alexander might even be drunk during the game.

There was a little delay before anybody came out of the bullpen, which was so far down the left-field corner you could hardly see it. I yelled "Alexander," and when he didn't come out real quick people thought he was asleep or something. Then he came out, walking real slouchy-like. Alexander could have been drunk for all I cared, but he certainly wasn't. Hell, I'd rather have him pitch a crucial game for me drunk than anyone I've ever known sober. He was that good.

The guy was running around in front of the grandstand with that megaphone yelling, "Alexander now pitching for St. Louis."

I trotted about halfway out to the outfield to meet Alex. "Well, the bases are full," I told him, "Lazzeri's up and there ain't no place to put him." "Yeah," Alex drawled, "Well, guess I'll have to take care of him then." Alex threw only 3 warm-up pitches. He didn't need to throw 15 or 20 minutes like most pitchers to get warmed up. Then he fixed his little cap, fooled around with his belt, and looked to see if everybody was ready.

One big mistake in the World Series can decide the game—and brand you a goat for years.

My War with Baseball

Alexander's first pitch to Lazzeri was wide for a ball. Lazzeri took the next one for a strike. Then Lazzeri laid into the third pitch and it was a home run all the way. The Yankees were on top of the dugout steps to run and meet Lazzeri at home plate. And I was going to be the biggest bum in the history of the World Series. I knew it, too. But just before the ball went into the left-field stands, where it was supposed to go, we got a break. The wind pushed the ball a little more to the left. Enough left to make the drive foul by about 10 inches.

Then Alexander took care of Lazzeri like he said he would. He struck Tony out on a curve. And Alexander didn't let anybody get on base in the eighth inning, retiring the tail end of the line-up in order. He got the first two Yankees, Combs and Koenig, in the ninth inning. But the tough part was next—Ruth, Meusel and Gehrig.

Alex worked the corners carefully on Ruth and had a 3-2 count on him. Alex had better control than anyone in history. He wouldn't walk over a half-dozen batters all year unintentionally. Then he thought he caught the outside corner of the plate with a curve and started off the mound. But the umpire, George Hildebrand, called it ball four. Ruth got his twelfth walk of the Series.

"What's wrong with it, anyway?" Alex hollered at the umpire.

"Missed by this much, Alex," the umpire said, holding out his hands to show it had missed by 4 or 5 inches.

"For that much," Alex said, "you might have given an old sonofagun like me a break."

Nobody Wins the World Series

Meusel was up. He hit .320 during the regular season and could hit the ball out of the park to either field. The Babe was the tying run, standing over on first base.

Alex came in with a low curve to Meusel. Then it happened.

Babe Ruth, the slowest regular on the Yankees and a guy who ran like he was pulling a trailer, was trying to steal second.

Bob O'Farrell, my catcher, made a perfect throw to me at second base and I just held my glove out. Babe slid right into it for the final out. We were the World Champions. Babe Ruth saw to that—it was the only mistake I ever heard of his making in about 25 years of baseball. After Ruth was out he got up and shook my hand to congratulate me.

For years, sportswriters said that Ruth probably thought there was only one out. And Miller Huggins, the Yankee manager, said he sure didn't give Ruth any signal to steal. "That's right," Babe said later. "Nobody did anything. I just decided to go. So I went."

I'd have to say that luck, breaks, and mistakes by the other team—like Ruth's boner—decide World Series more than anything. Why? Well, for one reason, a World Series is so much different from anything a player has ever done, including being in an all-star game. It's a player's lifetime dream. It puts him under a terrific nervous strain.

I have no way of telling which players have felt the tension most, but I can confidently say that I feel everyone has butterflies in his stomach all during a Series and reacts differently. I heard one ballplayer say that "anybody who says he isn't nervous or excited in a World Series is either crazy or a liar." He's right, too. I've seen pinch hitters—even good regular hitters—strike out on pitches they never would have gone after during the regular season. They're pressing. They don't want to be called out on strikes in the World Series.

Bill Dickey, the former Yankee coach and a great catcher, tells a story about going out to the mound one time to talk to Monte Pearson, a standout pitcher, and that Pearson was too nervous to even get any words out of his mouth. Pearson was so good he pitched the Yankees to 4 straight pennants in 1936-39.

The stars are just as nervous—maybe even more so—than the so-so players. In 1917 pitcher Red Faber, who won 3 World Series games for the Chicago White Sox, stole third base with his teammate, Buck Weaver, already on it. In 1925 Roger Peckinpaugh, the shortstop of the Washington Senators and the most valuable player in the American League, made 8 errors—most of them on simple plays. In 1936 Lou Gehrig of the Yankees froze at third base and didn't even come in home for an easy run on a base hit.

Dick Groat's experience in the first game of the 1960 World Series against the Yankees is a good example of how players react to this stage fright. Groat was the Pirate team captain, the National League's Most Valuable Player, and batting champion. In the first inning Groat followed Bill Virdon, his roommate and leadoff man for the Pirates, who had walked. Groat admitted that he was so scared he nearly froze and just scratched his foot in the batter's box. The trouble was that scratching your foot in the batter's box was the Pirates' signal for the hit-and-run play. When Groat realized what he had done, he

Nobody Wins the World Series

jumped back and rubbed his forehead, which was the signal to kill the previous signal.

But Virdon was nervous, too. He didn't catch Groat's new signal and tore out for second base. Catcher Yogi Berra's throw to second was perfect, but Bobby Richardson, the second baseman, and Tony Kubek, the shortstop, must have been nervous, too. They forgot to cover second and Virdon ended up on third. Groat got a double and the Pirates scored 3 runs in that inning, which came in handy—they won by 2 runs.

I've heard lots of people claim the Yankees would have beaten the Cincinnati Reds in the 1961 World Series regardless of any bad breaks they might have had. Not in my opinion. The Yankees were lucky that somebody didn't hit a line drive a few feet to the left or right of Mickey Mantle for the 13 innings he hobbled around trying to play. You have to give Mantle credit for wanting to play, but if anything had been hit that he would have had to chase any distance the Reds probably would have won the game.

Take the third game, which is the one that gave New York a 2-1 edge over the Reds. They claim Maris' home run—his first hit in the series—was the turning point. The Reds were leading 1-0 in the seventh and Bob Purkey was working his way out of a jam. Got Maris on a simple fly and struck out Mantle. Yogi Berra hit a simple fly too, and Frank Robinson, the centerfielder, trotted in to catch it. Only Elio Chacon, the second baseman, wanted to catch it, too. Instead of either one of them catching the ball they banged into each other and the Yankees tied the score 1-1. It was important 2 innings later. The Yankees Won by one run.

My War with Baseball

I've heard people say that a boner decided the 1929 World Series that I played in for the Chicago Cubs. We were behind 2-1 in games won and lost, but had the Philadelphia Athletics 8-0 in the seventh inning of the fourth game. Al Simmons led off the Athletics' inning with a home run, but we got the next 2 batters out. Two A's got on base, then Mule Haas hit a long drive to right centerfield, which is one of the worst places in the world to catch a ball. It's a bad sun spot. Hack Wilson, our centerfielder, started in on the ball, then jumped back and saw the ball fall and roll for an inside-the-park home run that scored 3 runs. The Athletics went on to score 10 runs in that inning which was a record, and beat us 10-8. I've heard many stories about Hack's forgetting his sunglasses and losing the ball in the sun.

But I don't think that's the truth. Wilson wasn't my favorite player. I didn't approve of the way he drank and broke training, but I still claim that too much blame was placed on him for that incident. People forget, I guess, that he led both teams in hitting in the Series with a .477 average.

In my opinion Norm McMillan let 2 balls that he should have caught get through him for hits at third base. And if he had made those 2 plays the side would have been retired and there wouldn't have been any ball hit to Wilson.

The A's pulled the same kind of rally 2 days later to win the Series, and nobody can call them lucky on that. We led the A's 2-0 going into the ninth. Pat Malone, our pitcher, got pinch hitter Walter French out. Then Max Bishop singled. Haas hit a home run nobody could question—over the fence—and that tied up the ball game. Then after Mickey Cochrane made the second out,

Nobody Wins the World Series

Simmons doubled. Jimmy Foxx was intentionally walked to get to Bing Miller. Miller hit a double to win the game—and World Series—for the A's.

Through the years one play like Wilson's seems to brand a player a goat. The 1941 Yankee-Dodger Series is probably the most famous. The Dodgers led the Yankees 4-3 in the ninth inning of the fourth game. Hugh Casey, a darn good relief pitcher, had 2 outs and 2 strikes on Tommy Henrich. Hugh just needed one pitch to end the game and he put everything he could behind it. It was a helluva good breaking pitch—so good the Yankees yelled "spitter"—and Henrich missed it for the third out. Mickey Owen, the catcher, missed it, too. Henrich made it to first and the Yankees got 4 runs to win 7-4.

Exactly 10 World Series earlier, the same play happened and nobody ever mentioned it again. The Cardinals led the Philadelphia Athletics 2-0 in the second game of the 1931 World Series with Bill Hallahan pitching for the Cards. It was the ninth inning. Hallahan had 2 outs and 2 strikes on Jim Moore, who was batting for Moose Earnshaw. Hallahan threw one past him, all right. The pitch also went by Catcher Jimmy Wilson and Moore got to first base. It didn't make any difference—Tilly Bishop, the next batter, fouled out to the catcher.

It's just not enough to have great players to win most World Series. You've got to work together as a team, because one mistake like those can mean the difference between winning and losing. During the regular season a team that plays solid baseball day in and day out will win over the long haul of 154 games, or 162 with the new 10-team schedules. The breaks, luck and mistakes will equal out in due time. That's why you see a .245 hitter leading the league with a .400 average in early May, then

My War with Baseball

fighting to hit .250 in August and keep from going back to the minors. That's why you see little guys like Bobby Richardson, a .265 hitter, going wild like he did in the 1960 and 1961 World Series; and big names like Maris failing to get the ball out of the infield the first two games and hitting .105 for the entire 1961 Series; guys like Billy Martin, a .257 hitter during the 1953 season, batting .500 in the Series while Mickey Mantle hit only .208.

My leading hitter in the 1926 World Series was Tommy Thevenow, the shortstop who hit .256 during the regular season. He batted .417 in the Series because he got the breaks. In the second game of the Series Tommy came up at a crucial time and hit a line drive down right field and straight toward Babe Ruth. Ruth tried to make a one-hand diving catch, but fell into the seats, and Tommy got a home run.

Now I'm not trying to take anything away from anybody. These players are hustlers, and this is one thing I always hammered away at my players. A guy can make his own breaks—by simple hustling. Some of the things Ruth did made him look like an idiot, but they sometimes created breaks, too.

The Cardinals and Tigers were all scoreless in the third inning of the seventh game of the 1934 World Series when Dizzy Dean, the Cardinal pitcher, got a single to left field. Most pitchers, especially in a tight game, don't exactly break their necks getting to first base on a clean single. So Goose Goslin, the Tiger left fielder, took his time and just lobbed the ball back into the infield. But Dizzy, a fellow I enjoy being on TV with occasionally, never slowed down until he was on second base. Safe, too.

That was important, believe me. Pepper Martin, the next hitter, bounced a ball down the first base line. If Dean had been on first, where first baseman Hank Greenberg would have been holding him on base, the play would have been a force at second. But Martin got a single, then stole second.

So, with daring men on second and third, manager Mickey Cochrane ordered Jake Rothrock put on intentionally. But by the time the Tigers got out of the inning the Cardinals had 7 runs—which took the wind out of Detroit—and won the game 11-0. That was the World Series.

I didn't think I gambled much in the 1926 World Series; my moves might have looked like gambling, but to me it was just playing my best men. Some managers, I guess, figure the other team has so much better personnel that they have to gamble to win. Especially in that first game, which I consider the most important one of the Series.

There are two ways of looking at one of the biggest gambles—the surprise starting pitchers. Some people claim this either means the manager doesn't have faith in his regular starters, or that his pitching isn't good enough to stop the other team and he has to gamble right off the bat.

A surprise pitcher beat us (Cubs) in the 1929 World Series, which was right before the stock-market crash that also surprised a few people. The Cubs was one of the greatest hitting teams in National League history. We had a team batting average of .303, and were loaded with such right-handed hitters as Kiki Cuyler, Hack Wilson,

My War with Baseball

Riggs Stephenson, Gabby Hartnett and myself. Charley Grimm was the only left-handed hitter.

We knew which Athletic pitchers we would have to face—Lefty Grove, George Earnshaw or Rube Walberg.

But Connie Mack, the Athletics manager, pulled a surprise and pitched thirty-five-year-old Howard Ehmke, who had pitched only 2 complete games and 55 innings all year long. Most of his baseball was behind him, and he hadn't even gotten into a game during the last 2 weeks of the season. The deal was, I learned later, that he had been scouting the Cubs during those 2 weeks.

None of us had figured on batting against Ehmke, who had a three-quarter side-arm delivery. Ehmke struck out 13 Cubs, which was a World Series record until Carl Erskine of the Dodgers struck out 14. Yankees in 1953; he beat our best pitcher, Charley Root, 3-1. It made Mr. Mack look like a smart gambler—he won.

But Ehmke got the breaks and I'm not taking anything away from him when I say that. He could have been a bum just as easily. In the first inning we got 2 men on base when I came up. I hit a fair ball straight for the right-field bleachers, which certainly meant that Ehmke was finished in this game. But the wind was blowing in off Lake Michigan, and the ball landed foul by just about as much as the ball Lazzeri hit against my Cardinals in 1926 and saved the Series for us. Then I struck out and we didn't score. The next time we faced Ehmke we knocked him out in the fourth inning.

For 3 straight World Series—1950-52—the National League managers gambled like Connie Mack did by using surprise pitchers against the Yankees. In 1950 Eddie Sawyer of the Philadelphia Phillies by-passed Robin

Nobody Wins the World Series

Roberts and some of his other regulars to start Jim Konstanty in the first game. Konstanty, who had made 74 appearances as a relief pitcher for a league record during the season, had never started a game during the 6 years he was in the big leagues. Sawyer's motive was simple: Roberts didn't feel like pitching. Sawyer almost won, too. Konstanty allowed only 4 hits, but Vic Raschi of the Yankees only gave up 2 hits and won 1-0.

In 1951 the Yankees expected to face either Larry Jansen, Hearn or Sal Maglie in the first game against the New York Giants.

Instead, Leo Durocher, who likes to gamble, started Dave Koslo. Koslo had gone 9 innings only 5 times all year. Leo wanted to "steal" a quick win and have his best pitchers available for the later games. He won the first— Koslo got it 5-1—but his big pitchers didn't produce later on, and the Yankees won the Series.

The following year the Brooklyn Dodgers pulled the same thing against the Yankees, hoping to catch them with a pitcher they weren't familiar with. The Yankees had batted against Billy Loes, Carl Erskine, Preacher Roe and some of the other Dodgers in previous World Series. But they had never seen Joe Black, a relief pitcher who hadn't been out of the minor leagues very long, and that's who they faced in the first game. Black didn't have a good fast ball, but he had a good enough slider and control. "We kept looking for the fast one," shortstop Phil Rizzuto said later, "but it never came." Black and the Dodgers won 6-5.

The practice of gambling with a new, unknown pitcher actually started before I ever began playing professional ball. In the 1909 World Series Manager Fred

My War with Baseball

Clarke of the Pittsburgh Pirates had the easiest job in the world in picking a pitcher to face the Detroit Tigers. He had Howard Camnitz, who had a 2 5-6 record; Lefty Leifield, 22-11; Nick Maddox, 13-8; veteran Sam Leever, 8-1; and Deacon Phillippe, who had won 3 games in the 1903 Series, was 8-3. The crowd booed when they read off the Pirates' starting line-up. The Pittsburgh pitcher was Charles (Babe) Adams, a rookie from Tipton, Indiana. Adams was scared—real scared. His first pitch went over the catcher's head. But he settled down and won 3 games, including a shutout in the final game.

John Heydler, who then was acting National League president, was probably responsible for Clarke by-passing his big pitchers and using a rookie. Heydler voluntarily told Clarke: "I saw this Detroit team stopped cold in Washington by Dolly Gray of the Senators. Gray pitches a lot like this new boy of yours—Adams. He'd give Washington trouble."

And these hunch selections have been going on ever since. Billy Southworth, who played right field on my 1926 Cardinal team, started rookie Ernie White against the New York Yankees in the 1942 Series when he was managing the Boston Braves. White beat them 2-0, and the Braves whipped the Yankees in the Series. The trick worked in reverse for Southworth 2 years later when he was managing the St. Louis Cardinals. Luke Sewell of the St. Louis Browns started Denny Galehouse, who had lost more games than he had won during the regular season and had the highest earned-run average on the team. Galehouse beat the Cards 2-1.

But I didn't play hunches with my pitchers in the Series. I pitched who I thought was best. Maybe Babe Ruth thought it might be best for him to steal second.

Nobody Wins the World Series

You never know in a Series—so don't ask me who's going to win. Or even who's going to lose.

12. How to Get in the Doghouse

ANY physically able American boy who doesn't play baseball is *not*, in my opinion, an American. I think it's just as important to learn to pitch, catch and hit a baseball as it is to learn history or the A B C's. Baseball should be a requirement in school. After all, it's our national pastime, isn't it?

I'm not claiming everyone should play professional ball. Or even try. But all boys should know the fundamentals. Some of the boys who play will love the game more than others. Some will stand out because they have more God-given ability than the others. They're the ones who are in professional baseball today.

If you're one of these boys, I envy you. You're in the greatest profession in the world. I also caution you. You're also in one of the most treacherous.

Take all the good advice you can get and try to get more. That's the only way you can be another Mantle or Maris. Whether you're one of the players on the New York Metropolitans or the Dothan, Alabama, Mudhens.

If you're in spring training with a major-league club, things look pretty good. There are other young players in camp, too. All nice guys. Or most of them. Some of these

All managers look for the hustling ballplayer.

How to Get in the Doghouse

players—maybe you—won't be with the club when it goes North to open the regular season.

I never buttered up to anyone to get ahead in baseball. Don't you, either. But don't get on the manager's "list" as lazy. Or have a don't-give-a-damn attitude. When I was managing the St. Louis Browns in 1952, a smart-aleck sportswriter who called me a slave driver wrote a little story about me. When a Browns rookie came in after about ten minutes of playing ball, he just pitched his glove aside and slouched down on the bench. The writer quoted me as saying, "Look at that damn kid, would you? No desire." And the next day, according to the writer, the kid was back down in the minor leagues.

I don't remember the circumstances in that particular case, but the point is this: all managers are looking for the hustling ballplayer. If they're trying to lead a team out of the second division, like I was with the Browns, then they are looking for hungry ballplayers who will give everything. That's their big hope—that they'll have players with a real spark. If you're on a team like the 1961 pennant winners, the Yankees and Redlegs, then they're looking for exactly the same kind of young players. Not that they're trying to replace the most valuable players in the leagues with you. But pennant winners have a tendency to get a little cocky the next year. Especially if a player knows there isn't anybody around to push him for his job. But if you're a hustler and get the job done, the manager is tickled to death to have you on the team. It makes the entire team hustle more.

I knew, when I took over the Browns in 1952, that the only way we could get out of the cellar was with hustling players. A hustler makes many of his own breaks. I looked for this type player. Jim Rivera, an outfielder who

225

got a late start in baseball and was at the age when most guys are giving up, was a rookie and one of the most exciting players in the American League that season. He beat people five different ways-—hitting, running, throwing, fielding and fighting. I said then, and I meant every word of it, that "Rivera was the only guy in baseball I'd pay my way in to see play."

The other guy I was impressed with was catcher Clint Courtney. Remember the incident about Clint in the chapter on cheating? Then you get the idea of how he helped the team. He was a hustler, out to beat somebody (managers don't stick around unless they win ball games). He'd spike his own grandmother if he thought it would help win.

I believe Enos Slaughter was one of the best hustlers on the field in the last 20 years. (I worked with him when I instructed Houston, the team he was managing, in 1960.) When Slaughter was thirty-nine years old and still in the majors he got a lot of razzing from young players. They called him "Grandpa," "Old-Timer" and "Phony," claiming he just hustled to show off. The last time I looked at Enos' batting average he was hitting over .400 as a player-manager for Raleigh in the Carolina league. Some of those bench warmers aren't hitting .275 in a lower classification.

There are other ways of getting into the manager's doghouse and getting something that the other players don't get—a plane ticket back to the minor leagues. I can't speak for each and every big-league manager—they've all got different dispositions—but many of them don't like comedians. I didn't want any part of them. Don't get me wrong. Comedians, and sometimes this includes players who are too cocky, are fine—if they can

How to Get in the Doghouse

produce and do everything that they claim to do. Few do; most don't.

Dizzy Dean did more popping off than anyone I ever heard about. Hell, they could have the best hitter in the league up and old Dizzy would laugh and say, "How'd you all like to see me strike him out?" Then if the manager turned his head, he'd mimic him. The whole team would laugh. There was nothing wrong with it in Dizzy's case—he was that good. Bobo Newsome, a pitcher I had drafted out of the Pacific Coast League for $7,500 for the St. Louis Browns and later sold to Washington for $40,000, did more clowning and silly stuff than people who work for the circus. Only when he and Dean clowned they always produced and it didn't hurt.

Newsome would go around saying, "just watch Ol' Bobo. Bobo'll win twenty games this season. Boys, just keep an eye on Bobo. That's Bobo now."

Or he'd always claim he had discovered the weaknesses of star players. Claimed he knew the inside on Joe DiMaggio, and wouldn't have any trouble with Joe the next time he faced him. DiMaggio got 3 doubles and a walk in 4 trips to the plate.

"That weakness, huh," Bobo said to somebody who needled him back, "why, man, it's doubles. Didn't you know that?"

I've heard that Dick Stuart, who hit 66 home runs for Lincoln in the Western League, came to the big leagues in 1957 and told everyone they could forget all about Babe Ruth's record. He, gentlemen, would personally see to it that he broke it. He did, all right. By adding up all his home runs hit in about 5 years. Don't be like that.

My War with Baseball

Now there's a slight difference between being a comedian like Dean, Newsome and Rabbit Maranville—who liked to slide between guys' legs—and having a know-it-all attitude like many rookies who come out of the minors and get a nice letter about reporting to the big-league club. And don't mistake cockiness for confidence. You've got to have confidence.

Some players can hit the long ball—like Stuart—and think that's all there is to hitting. I notice they usually replace Smart in some crucial games; like the final game of the 1960 World Series when manager Danny Murtaugh wanted somebody who could hit behind the runner, and things like that. Danny replaced Stuart with Rocky Nelson, who doesn't try to murder the ball and even hit a home run in that important game by just trying to meet the ball.

I'm not against long-ball hitters. You need players who do that. But rookies shouldn't think that all they have to do is hit home runs. They should learn in what parks it's to their advantage to try to hit home runs and in what parks they can't.

I'm not against a daredevil on the bases. If a manager has a kid who stole 55 bases at Amarillo, I'm certain he'd be pleased to get a good base runner. There's nothing more valuable in a tight pinch. But speed isn't everything, even if you're the fastest human in the world. If it was they'd hire 100-yard-dash men for base runners. Ty Cobb wasn't the fastest guy who ever played big-league ball, even if he holds the record for stolen bases. Good base running includes knowing when to steal, what pitchers to steal from, and how to get your break off them.

How to Get in the Doghouse

You learn to do this by watching, asking, doing, and above all having the right attitude: That you don't know it all because you hit .336 and 30 home runs for the Memphis Chicks.

If you have hit above .300, chances are you have been compared with me or even the 1961 American League batting champion. If you've hit 40 home runs or so with St. Cloud or Louisville, chances are you've been compared with Ruth, Maris and Mantle. Congratulations.

When you go to spring training you'll get all kinds of publicity. Some guy who played on your big-league team 8 or 10 years ago will be sitting next to a sports writer and he'll make sure you get a good story. He'll be quoted about you in the papers. You "can't miss," "you're the best rookie in 20 years," you'll hit "at least .315," you'll be "the rookie of the year—bar none," "you'll have more poise than anyone I've seen in a long time." And of course he's been around a long time.

This is really a lot nicer to clip out and mail to the folks back home than postcards with pictures of the hotel and statues in town where you're staying.

All this—I hope you know—doesn't get anyone in the big leagues. Managers don't let the newspapers pick their teams. In fact, this might make it a little harder—if you believe that you're sensational, that you're the new Rogers Hornsby or Babe Ruth, and if this leads you to believe all the stuff you read. After all, the sportswriters are pulling for the team you're on and they're partial.

I hope for your sake that you realize that the most publicized rookie in history gets a nice pat on the back, a real nice firm handshake, and a ticket to the minor leagues if he doesn't produce. In 1951 those newspaper guys wrote more nice things about a rookie named Mickey Mantle, who was jumping from Joplin, Missouri, to the New York Yankees, than they did about Joe DiMaggio.

And Mickey got a nice pat on the back, a real nice firm handshake, and a ticket to Kansas City, which wasn't in the big leagues then. Mickey had the determination to come back, and I hope you do too if this happens to you.

Speaking of the so-called minor leagues, they should quit referring to *all* baseball clubs outside of the major leagues as "minor." I don't claim that the Triple A teams are better than the majors; they aren't. But there are teams in the major leagues which could not win the pennant in some of the higher, so-called minor leagues. This is not the fault of the club owner, in my opinion, but because he can't buy or trade for or sign players who would improve the overall ability of his team. The farm clubs are responsible for this—where a rich major-league team can control players it can't use and won't even allow anyone else to use them in the majors.

A major-league club should not be allowed to control the contracts of more than 40 players, either directly or indirectly, through minor-league teams they own or have working agreements with. There is a rule that allows the big-league clubs to control the contract of a player for 7 years without the player being on the big-league roster. It's my honest opinion that 3 years is long enough. The way it is now it keeps players from advancing. Why shouldn't a player be allowed to advance himself if he gets the chance?

Jumping from some minor leagues to the majors as a rookie is almost as different as being safe or out. In the

How to Get in the Doghouse

minors you sometimes bat a week against pitchers with a decent fast ball, curve or control. Frankly, most of them simply are darn poor pitchers. At the most you don't face a top-notch pitcher over once every third or fourth day. Naturally you fatten your batting average, and people cheer every time you come to bat and the home team needs a run or two to get back into the game.

In the big leagues every pitcher is better and smarter than anyone you've been facing. If they weren't they'd be back down in the minors where you were playing. Do the same thing in the big leagues as you did in the minors and you just strike out. This, and I caution you here, causes more rookies' failures than anything. They just become excited, desperate, and start swinging at pitches they ordinarily wouldn't consider. When you go hitless for a long time you start pressing, and that ruins your timing. Timing, mind you, is 50 percent of hitting. You'll find that out. Then you feel lost at the plate, start seeking and getting advice about changing your stance and style. I want to underline this next sentence: *Don't suddenly change your batting stance because Ted Williams, Stan Musial, Roger Maris or Rogers Hornsby hit that way.* I mean that, whether you're going to be a regular on the New York Mets or you're trying to break in with Reno.

I sincerely hope that you have come as far as you have in baseball—I'm speaking of hitters now—because you've been hitting from a stance that has been the most natural to you.

You have batting coaches—and I've been a batting coach in the majors recently—who study you and determine what they think may be wrong with your hitting style—if you're going bad or aren't hitting.

My War with Baseball

I had an unusual experience along those lines the time I managed Beaumont to the 1950 Texas League pennant. My star player was a freckle-faced infielder named Gil McDougald, who led the league in the number of hits (187), had a batting average of .336, led in a bunch of other things and was the league's most valuable player. The New York Yankees, who owned McDougald, took him to spring training the following year.

Gil got some publicity as being a promising rookie, but I saw a quote or two in the paper about the Yankees not being sure that McDougald could make the big leagues with his stance. Gil did have one of the most unusual and unnatural stances anybody had ever seen. He put his right foot at the back corner of the batter's box, pointing out toward right field, with his left foot well back, sticking out toward third base. He almost looked like he was facing the pitcher. Just as the pitcher started to wind up, Gil would run his right hand down to the end of the bat. It looked like a washwoman's stance—but it was McDougald's natural stance and the best one for him.

I was driving out to Palm Springs to start spring training with Seattle when I heard about Gil. So I stopped in at the Yankee camp in Phoenix and advised Casey Stengel and his coaches not to change McDougald's style. They didn't, and McDougald not only became a regular on a pennant winner, but was the American League's Rookie of the Year.

Now that doesn't mean any stance a boy picks is best for him. When Miller Huggins, my first manager, told me that I was too light to swing from the end of the bat my first year in the majors and suggested I choke up on the bat, it was the right suggestion. The next year, after

How to Get in the Doghouse

I'd put on 30 pounds, he suggested that I start back in my own style because I was strong enough to get the bat around on big-league pitchers. He was right again.

If you're in spring training with, say, the Detroit Tigers, and playing in place of Norm Cash, Rocky Colavito, or Al Kaline, that doesn't mean manager Bob Scheffing thinks you're better than any of them. He merely wants to take a look at you—and this is your chance.

Rookies can get a distorted picture of the big leagues during spring training. A batter can go wild against second-string pitchers, and while they're pounding the daylights out of these guys, the proven veteran pitchers are just watching. So when the games start counting in the standings, the pitchers they face day in and day out have a pretty good line on your strengths and weaknesses.

There is no better way of making a strong showing in spring training than being in top condition. Some guys will be out of shape at the start of training—figuring to get in shape at camp—so you start with an edge by being in the right condition. The most important thing is building up your wind and having sound legs. That's 50 percent of the battle and is why so many guys fail. Obviously many players don't consider smoking as being harmful. But nothing cuts a player's wind more than smoking. Throw the cigarettes away, unless you'd rather be a fancy chain smoker than a ballplayer. In my opinion smoking hurts a player more than drinking. I feel so strong on smoking that I've turned down chances to make thousands of easy dollars for just allowing my name to be used on cigarette ads.

I know I sound old-fashioned—I am about baseball—but you can't get too much sleep in spring training. Take the attitude you're racing everyone else to the sack. Lay off the pizza and beer. Stick to steaks, potatoes, salads and milkshakes. If everybody else goes to a roadhouse, to hell with them. Nobody—especially a rookie—ever got a shot at the big leagues for anything he did in a roadhouse.

And if you do make it and you're a star, don't give the scandal sheets junk to write about. If you're determined to be a night owl and voluntarily shorten your career, then owl some place where it's good and dark. Now I'm not encouraging anyone to snake around—you shouldn't do anything you'd be ashamed of—but don't goof off where half the town can see you and gossip. Even if three or four young players and their wives want to go out for some clean fun they shouldn't go to a nightclub if they're going to touch anything that looks alcoholic. Even if it's free. You can pour yourself full of lemonade, and somebody will have you drinking gin like a fish and tell all about your blowing a ball game because you had a hangover.

You may be entirely innocent, but you can get the reputation of a boozer or rounder awful easy. Your value as a player goes down, regardless of what you do on the field, and that always hits you when it comes to talk about your salary.

And if you're playing baseball just for money I don't think you'll ever be any good in professional baseball. To succeed you've got to want to play the game more than anything. If you're offered a bonus I suggest you take every penny you can get. But don't also take on the attitude that you've got it made because you're fixed pretty good in the pocketbook. Money won't buy you base hits.

How to Get in the Doghouse

If you have signed for a bonus, even if it's a small one, there is a guaranteed way to make a lot of enemies and cause friction. Be sure and brag about your salary. There's a promising young outfielder in the American League who enjoys going around telling people all about his salary, which he puts up even higher than the exaggerated figure in the newspapers.

Don't try to show up anybody with a bunch of silly stuff. Like throwing your glove down to show up a manager if he takes you out of a game. Don't be a cry baby, which includes using the umpires as an alibi.

Sometime or other you'll get knocked down by pitchers. If you don't they don't respect you as a hitter. If somebody throws for your head be a man about it. There'll be times when you'd like to do something back at the pitcher. Don't worry about it. When your time comes up to get dusted off you should be able to take the good with the bad.

Remember most dusters are thrown to have an effect on the batter—to get him all excited. So don't go wild and help the pitcher. Even if he throws at you twice in a row, don't pay any attention to him. If you do he'll know the duster has an effect on you, and he'll spend more time trying to excite you. Don't charge out to the mound like Frank Robinson. What good does it do to get thrown out of a game? None, and it costs you money besides.

Don't be friendly with players on the opposing team. I never spoke to anyone on other teams unless they spoke first. Then I answered and didn't care if they spoke again. Regard everybody you play against as your enemy. Always keep the attitude that you're out there to beat the hell out of the other team because they're always trying

My War with Baseball

to beat the hell out of you. A pitcher is out there to get you out and you're out there to give him all the trouble you can. It's either you or him. I would always rather it be him on the losing end than me. And don't pay any attention to that silly thing about it's not whether you won or lost, but how you played the game. How you played the game. They keep score, don't they?

Don't squeeze everything you can out of baseball as a player. Make it your life, and never cheat on it for another business. Oh, I'm not saying a player shouldn't think about his old age and plan for some kind of business, but give baseball everything you have, and if you have anything else then use that energy for business. You've got lots less to worry about than when I played. We didn't have any Players' Associations or pensions. If you play the game right and hustle you'll always have a future in baseball.

If you're fortunate enough to be on a team that wins the pennant or World Series, or you're a standout in your first year and win all kinds of trophies, don't help the team slide back to second division the next year.

If you're a star or on a pennant-winning team you'll get invited to more banquets than you can attend. If the club wants you to attend, do it because that means it will usually help them. I know everything they put on those banquet plates looks good—people have been cooking all day for the thing. But you don't swing at every pitch you see in the majors, do you? Then you shouldn't eat all the stuff on your plate and show up all out of shape the next spring. I feel this hurt the Pirates in 1961. I read little newspaper stories all during the 1960-61 winter about the Pirates breaking just as many records on the banquet circuit as they did in the World Series. Well, they didn't get many invitations the next season. They guaranteed that by going to all those banquets and getting themselves out of shape.

There are other problems, too—like getting base hits or getting the batter out. But God gave everybody just so much ability, and if he gave you the ability to hit .210 and you hustled and hit .220 you've done a lot better job than the most talented guy in the world who hits .260. You don't have to be ashamed of anything. I've found out that it's a good thing not to have to hang your head.

13. My All-Time Team

I'D BE proud to be bat boy—on my all-time team. The team, which only lists players I've seen since 1915, would be so good it wouldn't need a manager. A couple of these greats were nearing the end of their careers when I played against them, but they were still better at their position than anyone I've ever seen since, or even heard about before. They are:

First Base—George Sisler—St. Louis Browns, Washington Senators, Boston Braves

Second Base—Eddie Collins—Philadelphia Athletics, Chicago White Sox

Shortstop—Honus Wagner—Pittsburgh Pirates

Third Base—Pie Traynor—Pittsburgh Pirates

Left Field—Babe Ruth—Boston Red Sox, New York Yankees

Center Field—Tris Speaker—Boston Red Sox, Cleveland Indians, Washington Senators, Philadelphia Athletics

Right Field—Ty Cobb—Detroit Tigers, Philadelphia Athletics

Catcher—Mickey Cochrane—Philadelphia Athletics, Detroit Tigers

"I threw a curve that hooked around the runner and smack into the catcher's mitt and he tagged the guy out."

My All-Time Team

Catcher—Gabby Hartnett—Chicago Cubs, New York Giants

Catcher—Bill Dickey—New York Yankees

Right-handed Pitcher—Grover Cleveland Alexander—Philadelphia Phillies, Chicago Cubs, St. Louis Cardinals

Right-handed Pitcher—Walter Johnson—Washington Senators

Left-handed Pitcher—Robert (Lefty) Grove—Philadelphia Athletics, Boston Red Sox

Left-handed Pitcher—Carl Hubbell—New York Giants

Now you don't see anybody who's playing today on that team; nor anybody who has played in the last 20 years. I know it's only natural for old-timers like myself to pick players from my era, but I also have respect for today's players. I think Warren Spahn, Ted Williams, Stan Musial and Joe DiMaggio are great players. But not quite as great as this team that I'd like to be bat boy for. The pitchers are my favorites. I never liked poor pitchers. I'd rather face great guys—Alexander and all the others in my day or even Spahn or Whitey Ford today—then all the rookies and second-string pitchers dead or alive. They knew what they could throw and they threw it better than anyone else. I knew what to expect and tried to hit it. I feel this is one reason why I hit so well against all the good guys. I never cared what the pitchers threw as long as it had zip. But the so-so pitchers who never used their heads—they're liable to throw anything.

Although I never batted against Walter Johnson regularly—he was in the opposite league—I'm convinced he absolutely had the best fast ball of anyone who ever played baseball. The first time I saw him was in 1917, when he was with the Washington Senators and I was a year or so away from my peak years with the Cardinals. Johnson, Ty Cobb, Casey Stengel and a bunch of us were on a major-league all-star barnstorming trip. We were playing in Kansas City, and Johnson's team, the American League All-Stars, led us 3-0. We had the bases loaded and Johnson had two strikes on me. He threw me a real fast ball and I knocked it straight for the fence. The ball hit the Bull Durham tobacco sign and happened to hit on a knot. The ball knocked out the knot and went through the fence for a home run and we won 4-3. The hole, I admit, was one of the biggest cases of pure luck I ever heard about. The long hit wasn't.

Most of the games Johnson lost were on long hits. You can't usually hit a slow ball or some dinky little pitch very far. Apparently most of the batters in the American League, where Walter did his pitching, didn't like to hit fast balls. He really mowed them down.

They talk about guys today being great because they win 20 games. Johnson—they called him "Big Train"—averaged over 20 wins a season in the 21 years he pitched for the Senators between 1907 and 1927. He won 413 games and struck out 3,508 batters. He won those games with a team that was as certain to be in the second division then as the Phillies or Athletics are today. In fact they used to laugh about the Washington club: "Washington, first in war, first in peace, and dead last in the American League."

I was still a kid when Johnson pulled his greatest feat, but I heard plenty about it. In 1908, when he was twenty years old, he beat the New York Highlanders (now Yankees) 3-0 on just 6 hits on September 4, which happened to be a Friday. The next day, Saturday, Manager Joe Cantillon asked Walter how he felt.

"As good as always," he answered. "Why?"

"Want to pitch again today?" Cantillon asked.

"O.K. with me," Walter answered.

Johnson beat the Highlanders 6-0 on just 4 hits.

The next day was Sunday and they didn't allow Sunday baseball then. So Johnson just sat around the hotel lobby fooling away the day.

The next day was Labor Day and they had a double-header against the Highlanders. Walter pitched the first game of that double-header, too, beating the Highlanders 4-0 on just 2 hits. He only walked one batter in those 3 games. The joke was that he hid when Cantillon came into the clubhouse after the third game.

"Afraid he'd ask how I felt," Walter laughed, "and I'd have to pitch the second game."

Walter, who died at fifty-nine in December of 1946, was the George Washington of American League pitching. A right-hander, he had the size, six feet one, 200 pounds. He had the fast ball, he had the control, he had the guts, and he was never out of shape. The Senators could always count on him to be ready for the opening game. He pitched 14 of them, and in 1910 pitched a one-hitter that would have been a no-hitter except his right fielder stumbled chasing the ball and it fell for a ground-rule double.

Johnson never fooled around with cutting, nicking or doing anything to the ball like they did so much of in those days. He even threw the ball out of a game if it was

My War with Baseball

scuffed. He didn't have to do anything to the ball—except throw it. "He was even too much of a gentleman," said Ty Cobb, who played against him regularly, "to dust me off despite all the things I'd do to him. He never even griped." In my opinion Johnson was afraid he'd hit somebody and hurt them bad.

The Senator fans thought so much of Johnson that one time when he wasn't able to pitch a certain game, after the newspapers said he would, the fans threw score cards, cushions and bottles. Some even demanded their money back.

When a Washington scout first offered Johnson a tryout he wouldn't sign until the club guaranteed him train fare back to his California home. But about the only time he had trouble beating another pitcher was when he played against the Boston Red Sox. Boston had a pitcher named Babe Ruth who beat Walt 6 out of 8 times, including 3 games by 1-0 scores. Walt, though, beat everybody else.

It should be clear by now that I consider Grover Cleveland Alexander the greatest pitcher who ever lived, right-hander or left-hander, drunk or sober. He threw easily, but he had one of the fastest fast balls I ever saw. It sounds corny, I know, to say that old Alex could thread a needle. But he almost did.

One time during spring training with the Cubs when the sportswriters kept pestering Alex to say something exciting about his control, he decided to give them a demonstration. He warmed up with Bill Killefer, his old catcher with the Phillies and later one of my coaches with the Cardinals. Killefer stood behind the plate with a

My All-Time Team

gallon tomato can with the ends cut out of it. Alex warmed up for a good 10 minutes, maybe 15, by throwing through the can. Never missed once.

Alex's control was always this good. Even when he was a kid and lived on a farm near St. Paul, Nebraska, with his twelve brothers and one sister. His mother said he was "always throwing things—rocks or anything he could find." They had a lot of chickens and turkeys on the farm and it was his job to kill them any time they wanted one for Sunday dinner. Only Alex's mother claimed he never used a hatchet or ax like everybody else did. He'd just pick up a rock and hit the chicken in the head hard enough to kill it. The chickens and turkeys were running, too.

Sometimes though, he'd slip into town and get into a baseball game with the boys. Finally he got into professional baseball in 1909 by signing with the Galesburg, Illinois, team of the Illinois-Missouri League. For $15 a week. He pitched good enough to get a tryout with the Phillies and in his rookie year, 1911, he won 28 games. Nobody had ever done that as a rookie before and I'm certain nobody has ever done it since. Win 28 games as a rookie!

Alex's salary was then $250 a month, or $1,500 for the season, but he got a $500 raise after his outstanding season. Money, though, didn't mean as much to him as it did to the other players. He never bothered to count it, and they say that any time a player wanted to borrow a dollar or two he'd just go pick it up off of Alex's locker; Alex would never know it until he paid him back.

He was a 20 or 30 game winner at least 10 years, even though he pitched in the smallest park in the major leagues. For 5 straight years his earned run average was below 2.00. And they consider even an earned run average of 2 as phenomenal. His 1915 average was 1.22.

Alex, who was tall and lazy looking, won 373 games and lost 208, which is the greatest record in the history of the National League. He pitched in more games than anyone (696), and pitched 90 shutouts—16 of them in the 1916 season.

His career, of course, had its ups and downs. He had the reputation of being a drinker because he liked to drink with his friends and his friends included everybody from the governor of Pennsylvania to baseball fans, to the governor of Missouri.

Sportswriters always exaggerated their stories about Alex's drinking episodes, and this is one of the reasons the Cubs put him on the waivers list in 1926. I always felt the stories weren't nearly as true as people made out. So did Killefer. That's one reason we got Alex for the cheapest price in baseball, $4,000, and he helped the Cardinals win the pennant and the World Series. He stayed sober for me, although he wasn't one of those fellows who'd take an ax and break a beer barrel, or pour gin down a sink.

But drinking bouts made good exciting stories and all the writers like to have exciting stories. Alex even thought one newspaper story about his drinking was exciting. He looked up one day and smirked, "Good God, I was never as drunk as this fellow had to be who wrote this here story. You guys read this?"

Alexander's best years were behind him when he was traded to the Chicago Cubs after the 1917 season. And when he came back from the war he did drink more than ever. But liquor wasn't the main reason he acted up every now and then. He volunteered for World War I and was a sergeant with the 342nd Field Artillery unit of the 89th Infantry Division in France. Alex's job was to help fire one of those big guns against the Germans, and they say he even had better control with that than in the National League. But the guns made him deaf in one ear and a little hard of hearing in the other. After the War he had occasional attacks of epilepsy, and since this never was known too much it caused some people to think he was drunk when he wasn't. That was one of the reasons why he drank, his wife has said. She also said Alex always pitched better with a hangover.

Alex studied the hitters and knew their habits. He didn't always consider the catcher's signal as sacred. (It's not supposed to be, anyway—it's only a suggestion, and a pitcher should shake a catcher off if he doesn't agree with him.) If I or anybody else changed his stance enough to be thrown off by another pitch, Alex would throw a different pitch than the one the catcher signaled.

He didn't fool around out on the mound. On June 26, 1915, he threw only 76 pitches—an average of a little over 8 an inning—in beating Brooklyn 4-0. One time the Phillies had to catch a train, and there wasn't going to be much time to play the second game of a double-header. "There's time if we hurry this damn thing up," Alex said. He hardly stopped after the catcher fired the first ball back, and pitched the game in 59 minutes. Won it, too.

Although Alexander never pitched a no-hitter, he pitched as many as 4 one-hit games in a season. He won his 29th game of the season in the first game of a double-header on the first day of the 1916 season. He wanted to win 30 that year, so he pitched and won the second game. That was no freak. He pitched and won a doubleheader the next season, too.

I shared Alex's biggest thrill with him; pulling him out of the bullpen in the seventh game of the 1926 World Series to stop the Yankees and win the championship. He talked about that game until he died, of a heart attack, in November of 1950.

Everybody but Killefer and I had given up on him a couple of months before. The next year, when forty years old, he won 21 and lost 10. He was 16-9 the next season—his last good year. I wasn't with him during his last days in the majors, but I'm certain he was tough. Jack Sher wrote something in *Sport* magazine about it. "When Hornsby was traded to the Giants, some of Alex's heart went with him. He might have gone on another decade pitching for a manager like Hornsby, a guy who let him pitch his own game."

Naturally I let him pitch his own game. Why should I—or anyone else—tell the greatest pitcher who ever lived how to pitch?

About the time Walter Johnson was nearing the end of his playing career in 1927 National Leaguers like myself heard plenty about a left-hander with the Philadelphia Athletics who could throw a fast ball just about as well as Johnson. They were talking about Robert (Lefty) Grove, and I got to see what they meant two years later when he pitched against the Chicago Cubs which I was playing with in the 1929 World Series.

Grove had a fancy long windup with such a follow-through for his overhand fast ball that his hand almost touched the ground when he finished up. You realized

My All-Time Team

you had seen a fast ball when you batted against Grove, and I'd have to say he had the second fastest ball in all American League history and the fastest for a left-hander.

I didn't know him well like Alexander, but he was the type person nobody got to know very well. Besides, he was a lot like me. He wasn't a mixer, didn't care about joining the team in a big party. He liked to sit around the lobbies and smoke long cigars he'd buy from the mail order places.

All you had to do was look at his record to tell how good he was. After he had his first 20-game winning season in 1927, he won 20 or more games for 8 straight years, and pitched the Athletics to 3 straight pennants and 2 World Series championships. In 1931 he won 31 and lost only 4, once winning 16 straight games, and winning 4 games in 7 days. This was also during the era when the ball became a little more lively in the American League and Babe Ruth was knocking everything out of sight.

Grove could either start or relieve. During his great '31 season, he finished up a 1-0 win by striking out Ruth, Gehrig and Meusel; another time he relieved with the bases loaded in the ninth inning and struck out Ruth, Gehrig and Lazzeri on 10 pitches. Lazzeri fouled off a pitch.

Lefty, who now lives in Ohio, came out of the mountains and built up quite a reputation with the Baltimore Orioles which was then a minor-league team. After he struck out Ruth 9 times in 11 at-bats and didn't lose a game against the big-league clubs in spring training, he

My War with Baseball

became hot stuff. The Orioles sold Grove to Connie Mack and the A's after the 1924 season for $100,600.

Lefty had the habit of pitching too fast—just about as fast as he could get the ball back. It wasn't unusual for him to walk the bases full, causing Mr. Mack to come out to the mound and quiet him down, then strike out the side.

Mack had straightened him out by the time I faced him in the 1929 Series. Since he had pitched the A's to the pennant we had expected to see him as a starter, but that was the time Mack used Howard Ehmke in that famous surprise move. Grove relieved George Earnshaw with 2 out in the fifth inning of the second game and struck out 6 of us Cubs to save the win; when the A's got those record 10 runs in the seventh inning of the fourth game to go ahead of us 10-8, Grove came in and didn't allow a hit over the last 2 innings.

Lefty was also known as moody and hot-tempered, and the newspaper boys used to give him a going over for refusing to pose for pictures before a game. He always wanted his own way, they tell me. He led the Yankees by a run with 2 out and 2 on (first and second) in the ninth inning when he wanted to intentionally walk Gehrig, the next batter. When the catcher stepped out for Grove to lob the ball to him, Mack motioned not to walk him. So Lefty intentionally made a wild pitch, putting the runners on second and third.

Mack signaled for Grove to walk Gehrig. He did. Then struck out the next batter.

They tell about the time Lefty was pitching for the Boston Red Sox and lost a game on shortstop Joe Cronin's error. After the game Lefty really chewed out

My All-Time Team

Cronin, as he usually chewed out anybody who cost him a game. But Cronin, in this instance, was his manager.

Lefty loved to win, hated to lose and hated to quit. He didn't quit until he won his 300th game in 1941, which is something nobody else could do until Warren Spahn won his 300th game 20 years later.

That's why Grove's won-lost percentage of .682 is the highest in the Hall of Fame.

Pitchers are scouted and signed because they have a good fast ball, or good curve and control. Yet you'll see pitchers spending half their lives fooling with a dinky little curve—that thing they call the slider. Or trying something new.

Maybe Carl Hubbell is partly responsible for that. In 1926 the Tigers had a young left-handed pitcher named Hubbell who kept fooling around with a pitch called the screwball. Most people hadn't even heard of it, and lots of big leaguers told him he would ruin his arm. In fact Cobb, who was the Tiger manager, didn't think enough of Hubbell to ever let him appear in a big-league game. The Tigers, who owned his contract, sent him to Toronto of the International League, and then eventually down to Decatur of the Three-I League. Hubbell was released outright to Beaumont, and Beaumont sold him to the New York Giants.

But Hubbell, a tall, thin, easygoing guy, developed the best screwball I ever saw and won 62.2 percent of his major-league games with it. He won so often and so consistently with his screwball that they called him the Giants' Meal Ticket. (A screwball is just about as hard to describe as it is to hit. Hubbell's screwball had sort of an

My War with Baseball

"out drop" on it, which caused the ball to be hit into the ground a lot. Lou Gehrig described it pretty well once: "You never know when it's coming, and when it does come you don't know what to do with it.")

Hubbell had the control to do about anything he wanted. He had the theory that he would make the batter hit the pitch he wanted him to hit. It evidently was pretty good—he was the National League's most valuable player twice. One of those years was in 1933, when I was back with the Cardinals and near the end of my playing days. We played the Giants in a double-header in the Polo Grounds on July 2. Hubbell pitched the first game. The game went 18 innings and Carl beat us 1-0, on 6 hits, didn't give up a walk—which also meant he pitched 12 perfect innings. That year he won 23 games, had a 1.66 earned run average, pitched 46½ consecutive scoreless innings, had 10 shutouts, and beat the Senators twice in the World Series. He only walked 47 men in 309 innings.

He won 16 straight games without a loss in the last part of the 1936 season and extended that streak to 24 by winning the first 8 games the following season.

Despite all of Carl's exploits—which included 2 no-hit games—his greatest performance came in the 1934 All-Star Game in the Polo Grounds. Carl opened for the National League, and the first batter, Charley Gehringer of the Tigers, got a single and went to second on an error. Then Carl walked Heinie Manush. Babe Ruth was up and Carl was already in trouble.

Hubbell threw 3 straight screwballs to Ruth, and Ruth didn't take his bat off his shoulder. All 3 pitches fooled Ruth and he was called out on strikes.

My All-Time Team

Lou Gehrig was up next. Gehrig had a 1-2 count on him. Hubbell threw him a screwball and Lou went down swinging, for the second out.

Jimmy Foxx, a right-handed hitter, came up. Gehringer and Manush pulled a double steal on the first pitch, which was a called strike. Foxx fouled off the second pitch and missed the third, for the third out.

Then in the top of the second, Hubbell struck out Al Simmons, one of the game's great hitters, and Joe Cronin for 5 strike-outs in a row. Bill Dickey got a single to break his strike-out streak; then Carl struck out Lefty Gomez—making that 6 strike-outs against 7 All-Star players.

Carl kept on like this until he won 253 games, and he didn't want to quit. He wanted to pitch in 1944, but he was almost forty years old, his arm had to be operated on, and he would have had trouble getting his arm into shape anyway since it was a war year and the ball clubs couldn't take spring training in the South. So the Giants made Hubbell the director of their farm system just before Christmas in 1943. And ever since the Giants have had one of the best farm systems in baseball.

I used to play against George Sisler of the St. Louis Browns every spring and fall in the St. Louis City Series exhibitions, and feel he is the greatest fielding first baseman I ever saw or played against. Which should make him the No. 1 first baseman of all time since he had a batting average of .341 over 16 seasons, got 2,812 hits, and his .420 batting average in 1922 ties him with Cobb for third behind my .424. He could hit hard to all fields and was an exceptionally good base runner.

During his 16 seasons George had a fielding average of .987. Which isn't bad, since Hal Chase, who is considered the fanciest fielding first baseman of all time by most, hit .291 and had a fielding average of .980.

Besides playing in the same town George and I had a lot in common. I worked a lot with Branch Rickey, and Rickey discovered Sisler when he was a student at the University of Michigan. George played about everything at Michigan, where Rickey was athletic director, including third base—despite being left-handed. He started in professional baseball as a pitcher and came up to the Browns in 1915—the same year I broke in with the Cardinals.

George, who is five-eleven and weighed around 170 pounds, originally signed a contract with the Pirates. At the same time, however, his father signed one for George with the Browns. There was an argument and the Browns got him in the official ruling by the commissioner's office.

Sisler had some trouble with his eyes—kept having blind spots and all—and stayed out of baseball for the 1923 season. But he came back and had such seasons as .345, .340 and .327. As it was, George hit .341 and if he hadn't had the eye trouble he would probably have a higher average than Cobb's .361.

I'm listed at second base on just about every all-time team, but like most people I'm not going to be an egomaniac and pick myself at second. My vote here goes to Eddie Collins, a jump-type little guy whom people called "cocky" but who I feel just had more confidence than anything.

My All-Time Team

Eddie, who was one of the finest hit-and-run batters I ever saw or played against, was the first of the college boys to make good in the big leagues. He played football and baseball for Columbia and somehow or other caught the eye of Connie Mack of the Philadelphia Athletics. Mack wanted Collins to play for the A's and Collins wanted to play for both the A's and Columbia, which was impossible. But Mack solved that. Eddie Collins entered professional baseball on September 17, 1906, the records show, as "Eddie Sullivan." (Edward T. Sullivan on the contract.) He got a single off Big Ed Walsh and didn't make any errors fielding.

The plot eventually was uncovered, so after he graduated he began playing pro ball under his own name. The players, though, still thought of him as "Sully." Mack tried Collins in right field, but he played that worse than Babe Herman. He finally found a natural position, second base, and he practically revolutionized play around that position. Billy Evans, a great umpire, once remarked: "Collins was the quickest thinker I ever saw with a ball."

He was even better as a hitter—averaging .333 over 25 seasons with the Athletics and Chicago White Sox. He led the Athletics to 4 pennants in 5 years from 1910 to 1914, and when I broke into the majors and was shifted to second base, I really admired Collins when I played\ against him in spring-training exhibition games.

When he was traded to the White Sox in 1915 Collins balked and refused to go at first. He finally did and became just as famous with the White Sox, helping lead them to 2 pennants. Although he got 9 hits in 22 at-bats for a .409 average in the 1917 Series against the Giants,

My War with Baseball

he is best remembered for a rare "bonehead" play in which he came out as a hero.

The White Sox were leading the Giants 3 games to 2 and the sixth game was all tied up. In the fourth inning Collins got on base on an error, and went to third on Joe Jackson's single.

Hap Felsch hit a ball back to the pitcher, and Collins took a bigger-than-usual lead off third base to draw a throw and keep the Giants from making a double play. Collins fooled Cy Benton, the Giant pitcher, so much that Benton thought he was going to the plate, and whirled and threw to the catcher, Bill Riordan. Collins started back to third with Heinie Zimmerman, the third baseman, behind him. Collins danced back and forth a couple of times. The catcher threw to Zimmerman and stepped about a foot out of the base line. But nobody was covering home plate and Zimmerman ended up chasing Collins across the plate with the winning run.

Collins played in the 1919 World Series against the Reds, but that was the one marred by the famous Black Sox scandal. (Collins wasn't involved.) The scandal really rocked the White Sox, and the accused players were barred for life. The White Sox didn't have much heart the next season, but Collins must have had more than the others because he batted .369.

Eddie, who died in 1951, also became manager of the White Sox and vice-president, treasurer and business manager of the Red Sox. And he was voted into the Hall of Fame in 1939 mostly because of his hitting and fielding. But he was a base runner, too. His spikes weren't as sharp as Cobb's, but he stole 744 bases, including 81 in one season (1910). All you had to do was see the games he played on September 11 and 22, 1912. He stole 6 bases in each game. It was, still is and always will be the record.

When I found somebody to play a game with as a kid around Fort Worth I wanted to be a shortstop. Like the Pittsburgh Pirate star, Honus Wagner, who won 8 batting championships and led the National League in just about everything but home runs. By the time I got to the majors Mr. Wagner was forty-one years old, wasn't playing every game, and they told me he had "slowed up quite a bit." Still, he's the best shortstop I ever saw in baseball. John McGraw, who saw Honus all through his career, said, "Wagner was the greatest all-around player who ever lived."

A right-handed batter, Wagner weighed 200 pounds, was bowlegged, had a barrel-like chest and looked sort of like an ape. He had the reputation of being a clown, and he wasn't trying to be a clown. He went to work digging coal in the mines when he was twelve and he was as tough as they come in baseball. He never gave ground to anybody who tried to cut him down. He had all kinds of scars from spike wounds. He treated cuts with tobacco juice. Cobb remarked in 1910 that Wagner was the only man he couldn't scare. Cobb probably should have been scared of him.

In the 1909 World Series Cobb singled and hollered to Wagner, "I'll be down on the next pitch, you left-footed clown."

"Dutchman'll be there, sonny boy," Wagner yelled back.

They were both right. Cobb went to second and Wagner was there.

Cobb slid into second trying to bust up Wagner, but Honus made a fancy sidestep and tagged Ty right in the mouth.

Honus could do about everything. I've never heard anybody say they saw Honus throw to the wrong base or make the wrong play. He led the National League in hitting with averages of .381, .355, .349, .350, .354, .339 and .334; he batted over .300 for 17 straight years and had a career average of .329; he stole 720 bases and stole 61 of them the season he was thirty-four years old.

Although he led the Pirates to 3 pennants, Honus talked about one game against the Cubs more than any other. The Pirates were behind a run in the eighth inning. Tommy Leach was on second, with 2 out for the Pirates and Wagner at bat. Frank Chance, the Cubs manager, told his pitcher to walk Wagner. Honus got mad. He lunged across the plate and poked a ball into right field to score Leach. He stole second, third and home on the next 3 pitches.

He never got more than $10,000 any season for all of this kind of play.

He would go to spring training with the Pirates every year until he died in 1960. He was one of the best storytellers of all times. He'd maintain that today's players are even better than in the old days because they're smarter.

He could hit to all fields and he did the same thing with his stories that kept the players laughing. He liked to tell about an outfielder who played in the "old days" and had the strongest arm he had ever heard about.

"The home team was at bat with the score tied in the last of the ninth," Wagner was saying, "when the guy hit a ball four hundred and sixty-five feet to the centerfield wall. Looked like the run would score from third easy."

"This guy really threw him out?" a rookie asked.

"First he made the catch," Wagner said, "then drew back with all his might to throw. But he knocked a hole in the fence, and his arm got caught in the hole."

When Honus first started with the Pirates they played in a park that was bordered by a railroad, for sure. Wagner had a story for that, too. "I hit a ball over the fence just as the train was passing," Honus once said, "and the ball went down the smokestack. But the engine went puff-puff and blew the ball right back over the fence. Danged if the left fielder didn't catch the ball."

Then there was one about Wagner's greatest play. "We had the runner trapped behind home and third, see," he said, "and I was covering third. When I got the ball the runner got between me and the catcher so I couldn't throw to the catcher without hitting him."

"What'd you do, Mr. Wagner?"

"Oh, I got him out," he grinned. "Threw a curve that hooked around the runner and smack into the catcher's mitt and he tagged the guy out. Sure taught him a lesson."

Wagner did everything the best.

Four years after Wagner retired, the Pirates had another infield star—Harold (Pie) Traynor. Pie never won a batting championship. And there've been some outstanding third basemen through the years—Larry Gardner, Heinie Groh, Joe Dugan, John McGraw, Red Rolfe

My War with Baseball

and George Kell. Some were good hitters, some were good base runners, throwers and fielders. I didn't see all of these third basemen, but I still maintain that Traynor was the best third baseman I ever saw doing all of these things.

He wasn't what they call "colorful." But he was good. I played against him for a dozen years. I watched him lead the Pirates to the 1925 World Series—the year before my Cardinals won. He could dig the hot grounders out of the dirt, he could run and he could hit. He hit steady and had an average of .320 during his 17 years with the Pirates.

Pie, who got his nickname for ordering pie at a store when he was a kid around Boston, wanted to play for either the Braves or Red Sox. But Portsmouth, which gave him his start in pro ball, sold him to the Pirates and there wasn't much room for shortstop Traynor when he came to the Pirates since Rabbit Maranville was playing short. They moved Pie to third and he was the best man they ever had there.

I can't separate the top 3 catchers—Bill Dickey and Mickey Cochrane, who batted left-handed, and Gabby Hartnett, a right-handed hitter. I'm more familiar with Hartnett, whom I played with and managed on the Cubs and who runs a bowling alley in Chicago not too far from where I live. Gabby, who weighed 220 and stood six foot one, hit with power and had a good average of .297 from 1922 to 1940.

Of all the things he did he is still remembered for his "Home Run in the Dark"—that's what I think they call it. In September, 1938, which was a couple of months after

My All-Time Team

Gabby became manager of the Cubs, the Pirates came to Wrigley Field to sew up the pennant. They had already built a new press box to take care of all the sports writers who wanted to cover the World Series. The Pirates only needed one win in the 3-game series to practically clinch the pennant. This day they were trying to get that one win in the third game because they had already lost the first 2. The score was tied 5-5 in the bottom of the ninth and it was getting so dark this was the last inning. Mace Brown had 2 outs and an 0-2 count on Hartnett. Instead of wasting a pitch, Brown tried to slip a third strike past Gabby in the dim light and Gabby knocked the ball over the fence where all the ivy is.

Dickey, who batted .313 and hit 202 home runs in 17 seasons with the Yankees, had one of the strongest arms I ever saw. He blocked the plate with the best. He wasn't dirty, but he didn't let anyone run over him. One day Carl Reynolds, a Washington outfielder, had the play at the plate beat easy, but clobbered Dickey, knocking him about 15 feet. Dickey walked straight for the dugout and hit Reynolds so hard in the jaw that nurses had to feed him through a tube for the next month. Dickey was suspended for a month and fined $1,000. That was his only fight.

Bill didn't always want to be a catcher. When he was a kid around Hot Springs he and another boy named Jimmy Froley both wanted to be pitchers on the same team. So they'd take turns pitching and catching. Bill caught on with Little Rock of the American Association in 1925, and in 1928 the Yankees brought up two rookies—Dickey and Leo Durocher—who spent more time on the bench than on the field. The next year, twenty-two-year-old Dickey was the Yankees No. 1 catcher. He stayed there—catching over 200 games a year for a record 13 years—until he got back from the Army in 1946 and managed the Yankees that season.

When Casey Stengel became the Yankees' manager in 1949, Casey hired Dickey as coach, especially to teach a funny-looking little guy named Larry Berra. A lot must have rubbed off on Larry (Yogi) Berra.

There are plenty of people who claim Mickey Cochrane was the greatest catcher who ever played. Truthfully, you can get too many arguments against that. He had power, and besides, batted .320 in the 13 seasons he played for the Philadelphia Athletics and Detroit Tigers; he caught at least 100 games for the first 11 straight years.

Mickey, I found out playing against him in the 1929 World Series, was the kind of man you need catching. He was fiery; he was a take-charge guy. If he thought the pitcher wasn't putting out he'd charge out to the mound and chew him out. He didn't mind fighting, either.

He was sort of a lone wolf like me. He didn't go to all the parties or run around with all the players to shows and things. He stayed in shape to play baseball. It paid off, too. In 1929-31 he hit .331, .357 and .349 in leading the Athletics to 3 straight pennants and 2 World Series championships.

After Connie Mack lost some money in the stock-market crash, he needed money and sold Mickey to the Detroit Tigers in December, 1933, for $100,000 and catcher John Pasek. The Tigers thought enough of Mickey to make him manager, and he won the pennant

My All-Time Team

during his first two seasons managing the Tigers. On May 25, 1937, he was beaned by Irving (Bump) Hadley of the Yankees, had a triple skull fracture and almost died. He came back in 1938 as nonplaying manager.

They call my all-time outfield of Tris Speaker, Babe Ruth and Ty Cobb the "American League's Dream Outfield." These three players are the best in either league, believe me.

Take Speaker. He didn't get much publicity as a hitter. He had to compete with Ruth and Cobb. He got all of his notices as a defensive man. Yet in 21 seasons from 1908 to 1928 with the Red Sox, Indians and Senators, he had a career batting average of .344. That's second only to Cobb as the American League's all-time best.

He was the greatest fielder I ever saw. Best anybody else ever saw, too. A centerfielder, Tris was known as the "Fifth Infielder." Playing before the lively ball, he played in almost behind the second baseman and could go back to catch a fly ball faster than anyone I ever saw. One time he even knocked himself out cold when he crashed into a wall. He still had the ball in his glove, though, when they brought him to. In both the 1909 and 1912 seasons he made 35 assists, which is—needless to say—a league record. He even made unassisted double plays—and remember he was an outfielder. That was in 1912 when he hit .383 and didn't even win the batting championship.

The Red Sox bought Tris from Houston for $750 in 1907, but after he went 2 for 19 for a .158 batting average they didn't even send him a contract for 1908. As a free agent he went to the Giant's camp and didn't get a second look. So he went to the Red Sox training quarters in Little Rock, and when the Red Sox broke camp they gave the Little Rock club Speaker for the rent on the stadium. Only stipulation was that if Speaker did make good the Red Sox got the first chance to buy him. Tris won the Southern Association batting championship with a .350 average that season, so the Red Sox bought him back for $500 in 1909. He later roomed with a pitcher, Babe Ruth, and they led the Red Sox to the 1915 pennant. (Tris had already played in the 1912 World Series.)

He was sold to the Cleveland Indians for $65,000 and a couple of players in 1916, but didn't want to go. He went, of course, and when he was named manager in 1920 put the Indians in the World Series.

Now Cobb—I've played against him in exhibitions and managed against him in the 1921 Winter League in California when he managed the San Francisco Seals and I managed the Los Angeles Angels. He was a helluva competitor. He wanted his own way, and Hugh Jennings, one of his managers, once said the only way to manage Cobb was to leave him alone. If Cobb didn't want to take batting or fielding practice he didn't.

But what was the use? He led the American League in stolen bases 6 times. Led the league in batting 12 times. And, as I've said all through this book, he was the greatest player I ever saw.

Now Babe Ruth. They may have written more about the Babe than about George Washington or Abraham Lincoln. All I can say new about Ruth is that he hit for power—not average—and had a lifetime batting average of .342. Dead ball or lively ball, he'd hit 60 home runs if they were pitching him softballs.

14. Cleaning the Bases

I NEVER liked to leave runners on base when I was swinging a bat. I find I haven't changed just because I'm swinging with a typewriter. So I'll answer a couple of questions people have asked me.

Someone wanted me to name major-league players who hated baseball. I can't do that because I don't think there are any. If there were and they were around me they wouldn't stay around long.

There are only two kinds of players as far as I'm concerned—the guys who put out and the guys who don't. The ones who played hard never had any trouble with me. The ones who didn't give me everything had trouble, and they'll always have trouble as long as they're around me.

So I can't say I ever knew a player that amounted to anything who hated baseball. If they've called me rough and hard-boiled and demanding, it's because I love the game and wanted to give my best to it and expected every player on the team to do the same.

Another question I've been asked is what it feels like when a player reaches the touchy point in his life when he has to decide—unless it's decided for him—that he's getting too old to play good ball. It's especially hard for a player who has been one of the best—a .330 hitter or so—and has got way below the .300 mark.

A magazine ran a story called "The Last Summers of Ted Williams and Stan Musial," figuring these two stars were finished players. Ted hit .254, which was the first time in 18 seasons in the big leagues he hit under .317; Musial hit .255, the first time also in 18 seasons that he had hit lower than .310 in the majors. Everybody figured age had caught up with them, but it hadn't. That's one of the reasons I rate Musial, Williams and DiMaggio as the only great hitters in the last 20 years. The next year, 1960, Williams closed out his career with a .316 average, which is remarkable for a forty-one-year-old man who was in two wars. Musial didn't do quite as well—hitting .275—but he didn't hang up his spikes. Not even in 1961 or 1962. These guys love baseball and want always to be in it.

Players' dispositions are so different that I never like to speak of them in general. Take DiMaggio. He played just as hard as Williams or Musial. But outside of serving as a coach for the Yankees in spring training last year for two weeks, which was more or less a vacation, he hasn't been connected with baseball since he retired at age thirty-five, after hitting .254.

But I know how Williams and Musial feel. Regardless of what players do after they stop playing, I don't think any of them ever get baseball out of their blood. You have to love it to play it right. If you don't play it right you don't stick around long enough to really love it. Especially the way I do.

I know I didn't want to quit playing. In fact I never wanted to be out of baseball any time after I started

Cleaning the Bases

playing professionally in 1914. That's why I took a job as Chicago scout for the New York Metropolitans just a few days after my sixty-fifth birthday. I've never been a scout before—but it keeps me close to the game I love. With the Cubs and the White Sox in Chicago there's a game almost every day. And I'm back at the ball park every day—where I feel I've always belonged.

HORNSBY'S RECORD

Playing Career

Year	Team	League	G.	R.	H.	2B	3B	HR.	RBI	B.A.
1914	Hugh-Denison	Texas-Okla.	113	47	91	12	3	3	...	.232
1915	Denison	Western Association	119	75	119	26	2	4	...	.277
1915	St. Louis	National	18	5	14	2	0	0	4	.246
1916	St. Louis	National	139	63	155	17	15	6	60	.313
1917	St. Louis	National	145	86	171	24	*17	8	70	.327
1918	St. Louis	National	115	51	117	19	11	5	59	.281
1919	St. Louis	National	138	68	163	15	9	8	68	.318
1920	St. Louis	National	149	96	*218	*44	20	9	94	*.370
1921	St. Louis	National	154	*131	*235	*44	**18	21	*126	*.397
1922	St. Louis	National	154	*141	*250	*46	14	*42	*152	*.401
1923	St. Louis	National	107	89	163	32	10	17	83	*.384
1924	St. Louis	National	143	121	*227	*43	14	25	94	*.424
1925	St. Louis	National	138	133	203	41	10	39	*143	*.403
1926	St. Louis	National	134	96	167	34	5	11	93	.317
1927	New York	National	155	133	205	32	9	26	125	.361
1928	Boston	National	140	99	188	42	7	21	94	*.387
1929	Chicago	National	*156	*156	229	47	7	40	149	.380
1930	Chicago	National	42	15	32	5	1	2	18	.308
1931	Chicago	National	100	64	118	37	1	16	90	.331
1932	Chicago	National	19	10	13	2	0	1	7	.224
1933	St. Louis	National	46	9	27	6	0	2	21	.325
1933	St. Louis	American	11	2	3	1	0	1	2	.333
1934	St. Louis	American	24	2	7	2	0	1	11	.304
1935	St. Louis	American	10	1	5	3	0	0	3	.208
1936	St. Louis	American	2	1	2	0	0	0	2	.400

	St. Louis							
1938	Baltimore	International	16	2	0	0	1	.074
1938	Chattanooga	Southern	3	1	9	0	2	.667
1940	Oklahoma City	Texas	1	0	1	0	0	1.000
	Major League Totals		2,259	1,579	2,930	541	168	302	1,579	.358

*Led League.
**Tied for Lead.

Major League Managing Career

Year	Team	Length	Finish
1925	St. Louis Nat'l League	4 months*	4
1926	St. Louis Nat'l League	Season	1
1928	Boston National League	5 months*	7
1930	Chicago National League	1 week	2
1931	Chicago National League	Season	3
1932	Chicago National League	5 months**	1
1933	St. Louis Amer. League	2½ months*	8
1934	St. Louis Amer. League	Season	6
1935	St. Louis Amer. League	Season	7
1936	St. Louis Amer. League	Season	7
1937	St. Louis Amer. League	4½ months**	8
1952	St. Louis Amer. League	3½ months**	7
1952	Cincinnati Nat'l League	2 months*	6
1953	Cincinnati Nat'l League	5½ months***	6

*Hired during season.
**Fired before season ended.
***Fired Sept. 17.

Made in the USA
Monee, IL
28 April 2026

49136205R00154